Mending the Nets

THEMES FROM FIRST JOHN

by

Pastor Bill Randles

And going on from there, He saw other two brethren, James the son of Zebedee, and John his brother, in a boat with Zebedee their father, mending their nets; and He called them.
(Matthew 4:21)

First published in Great Britain in 2000
by
St Matthew Publishing Ltd
Copyright © Bill Randles 2000
ISBN I 901546 0 9 8

Acknowledgements
Extracts from the Authorized Version of the Bible (The King James Bible), the rights in which are vested in the Crown, are reproduced by permission of the Crown's patentee, Cambridge University Press.

Cover picture by Su Shaw
© Su Shaw 2000

Further copies of this book are available in some bookshops or can be ordered from:
St Matthew Publishing Ltd, 24 Geldart St, Cambridge CB1 2LX   UK
Tel: +44 (0)1223 504871, Fax +44 (0)1223 512304
Email: PF.SMP@dial.pipex.com

CONTENTS

Other books by the same author:

Making War in the Heavenlies
Weighed and Found Wanting
Breaking down the Barriers (transcription of a talk)
Beware the New Prophets

Available from SMP Ltd

PREFACE

I have known pastor Bill Randles since 1995 when I first had permission to publish two books he wrote, *Weighed and Found Wanting* and *Making War in the Heavenlies*. Since that time we have met both here in the UK and at his church in Cedar Rapids, Iowa, where I had the great privilege to share fellowship and to preach.

His concern, from the heart, has been both to "snatch those from the burning" and to pastor and build up those who have been convicted of their errors and need the healing application of the Word.

This book is addressed to those who need nurturing in the Word of God. There truly is a "famine of the Word", yet it is a terrible sight to see people spiritually starving when they are still surrounded by plenty. There are no shortages of printed Bibles, as there are in some parts of the world, but there is a true shortage of godly and principled preachers and teachers of that Word. Far too many today do *"not endure sound doctrine; but after their own lusts they heap up to themselves teachers, having itching ears" (2 Timothy 4:3)*. And where there is demand you can always be sure there will be supply!

Bill Randles is one of the true teachers of the Word, *"rightly dividing the word of Truth."*

Philip Foster
*minister of St Matthew's Church Cambridge UK
and director of St Matthew Publishing Ltd*

Mending the Nets
Part I – THEMES FROM FIRST JOHN

Introduction

WHY JOHN WROTE

The Chinese pastor, author and martyr, Watchman Nee, in his book *What shall this man do?*, made an interesting observation about the careers of the three apostles, Peter, Paul and John. Nee observed that there is spiritual significance in the occupations that these three were engaged in when they were called by Jesus. We are told in Scripture that when Peter was called, he was busy as a fisherman, '*casting his nets into the sea*'. Paul happened to be a tentmaker by trade, crafting portable dwelling places. John, the beloved apostle, was also a fisherman, but when Jesus first called him he was on the shore with brother James, and they were mending their nets.

Furthermore, Nee observed that even the chronology of the ministries of these three is of significance. There is an order in which each of these three come into prominent ministry. Peter comes forth first, on the day of Pentecost, throwing out the net, preaching the Gospel boldly. It was also Peter, who was the first of the apostles to go directly to the Gentiles with the Word of the cross. The first half of the book of Acts features Peter prominently.

Paul comes next into prominent ministry. But his calling is different. It is true that Paul was an effective evangelist, but to him also was given revelation from Jesus Christ which became vital to the building of the house of God; the church which is the *'dwelling place of God in the Spirit'*. Paul was given the task of building the house of God, through the revelation given to him as a *'wise masterbuilder'* and steward of the mysteries of God. He was used to build upon the foundation which had already been laid – none other than Jesus Christ himself.

Finally at the end, John comes forth. He had been there at the beginning with Peter and the others, but not as prominently as Peter or Paul. He comes not to initiate as Peter, nor to build as Paul; his primary thrust is akin to 'repairing the nets'. John comes at the end of the New Testament, long after Peter has put down his nets and launched out into the Gentile world, and even after Paul has built the house of God through the revelation given to him. By the time of the last apostles, as Nee says in his book, '. . . but at the last, there are setbacks and disappointments. In his letter to the Philippians, Paul tells us why, "All seek their own, not the things which are Jesus Christ's" (Philippians 2:21).'

Selfishness wasn't the only problem. By the end of the first century, false concepts of Jesus, the gospel, and spirituality had threatened to completely redefine Christianity, to the point of obliterating the true gospel. The nets needed to be repaired.

John offers nothing new. His task is to call us back to that which is original, *that which was from the beginning . . . (I John 1:1)* that, living in this late hour, we might ' . . .*strengthen the things which remain . . .' (Revelation 3:2)*, that we might remain in "*Him that is true . . . even in His Son, Jesus Christ, the true God and eternal Life" (I John 5:20)*.

This is my twenty-second year of being a Christian, (which is more than half of my life). I have seen the times of great gathering, and modern day Peters in my lifetime have, *"launched out into the depths of the sea to let down their nets"*, gathering all, opening new doors and rejoicing in the possibilities. Having been a pastor since 1982, I can also surely appreciate the burden of many who, like Paul, have laboured to build up the house of God; *"the pillar and ground of the truth"*. How we still need the Peters and Pauls! I can also see that many of the nets have been frayed, dashed, and torn, and are in bad need of repair. The true, genuine Christian Gospel is again in danger of being distorted. Even the person of Christ Himself is being redefined in our generation. I agree with brother Nee that we need to have our nets repaired.

First John was written to counter a specific distortion of Christianity called *Gnosticism*. Gnosticism is a Greek term which relates to a special kind of elite knowledge. A *Gnostic* is a 'knowing one'. *(Gnosis* means to know, an a*gnostic* is one who claims not to know). What was it that these Gnostics knew? Their knowledge was supposedly the knowledge of God! They had set themselves up as the ones who "know God in a way far superior to the 'average Christian'". The Gnostics were impatient with the standard Christian teaching regarding the knowledge of God. It was just too simple and pedestrian. Good enough for uneducated peasants, slaves, and the disenfranchised people who made up the bulk of the Christian converts in the first century (see I Cor 1:25-26), but orthodox Christianity was far too plain for converted philosophers and intellectuals!

Think of it this way. Do you know God? *How* do you know Him? Have you ever seen Him? Have you ever heard His audible voice? Have you gotten beyond the Scriptures into a deeper intimacy with God, or are you still on the level of "mere head knowledge"? You say you love Jesus, but have you ever seen Him? Are you still waiting for Him to come and rescue you in some kind of an 'escape plan'? *

These and many others were the kinds of questions which the Gnostics would raise (and still do), thus unsettling the faith of the "ordinary Christians". After all, who wants to be just an "ordinary" Christian when you can be among the elite, in the "inner court" or on the cutting edge of the 'great move of God'! (Does this all sound familiar?) The Gnostics were far beyond the "mere head knowledge" of the so-called "average Christian". Through their esoteric visions, revelations, communications with angels, secret doctrines and elite hierarchies, they left other believers behind in their pursuit of "who they were" in the spirit realm. The faith of the average church member consisted of following the teachings of the apostles and of the Scriptures, sharing in the fellowship of the church, and patiently awaiting the *parousia* – which is the bodily coming of our Saviour from heaven – while enduring, in most cases, persecution, ridicule and scorn from this world. The Gnostics looked down on this in disdain, insisting that there had to be more for men of their insight! The result of the influence of these Gnostics was twofold. Many were drawn away into a counterfeit spirituality (the *"sin unto death"* – see page 107) by renouncing the real Jesus who came in the flesh, in order to embrace their own "Christhood". Others were severely weakened in their own faith, by contrasting their spirituality with the super-spirituality of these Gnostics. "Do I really know God? I thought I did until these people came along with their visions, revelations and secret teachings. I certainly haven't had the experiences these people claim to have: climbing the mountain of God, speaking with the different levels of angels, and learning that the Garden of Eden is actually inside of me! Who am I compared to these? These people really know God on an intimate level!"

We have the same problem today; Gnosticism in various forms has plagued the church for centuries. The "super-spiritual" have redefined the knowledge of God. An entire army of prophets, mystics, neo-

10

apostles and gnostics have been admitted into our churches and seminaries, and have in large part been successful in a redefinition of Christianity. This has not happened overnight. It has been a gradual but escalating process, and it has left few of the essential elements of Christianity untouched. The knowledge of God, the meaning of salvation, faith, prayer, spiritual warfare, and a host of other elements of the true Christian life have become "mysticised" and redefined.

For an outstanding example, take the subject of spiritual warfare. What has been understood to be the model of spiritual warfare as taught by the apostles? The battle has traditionally been understood to be one that consists primarily of ideas; our weapons have consisted of truth; the field is understood to be the arena of human thought — a battle for the minds of men!

"For though we walk in the flesh, we don't war after the flesh, for the weapons of our warfare are not carnal, but they are mighty through God, to the pulling down of strongholds, casting down vain imaginations, and every high thing that exalts itself against the knowledge of God, and bringing into captivity every thought to the obedience of Christ . . ." (II Corinthians 10:3-5.)

Paul and the other apostles waged the true spiritual warfare, in the book of Acts as they went forth debating, openly alleging, disputing and arguing in the marketplaces and synagogues that it is Jesus who is the Christ of God, the fulfilment of all that the Father has promised in the prophets. In Judea spiritual warfare meant reaching the minds of a Jewish audience, whose frame of reference was the Scriptures. To the larger Greek world, to whom Scripture meant little or nothing, and for whom concepts such as God, salvation and righteousness needed to be spelled out, spiritual warfare meant pressing the point that we are all made by the One True God, who made all things, and whose law is written on the heart of every man. Ignoring Him, making idols, therefore is inexcusable. Creation is a witness against it and so is your conscience! Spiritual warfare consisted primarily of daring to dismantle the wrong ideas – the intellectual, cultural, and emotional barriers that people cling to as "fig leaves" hiding from accountability to the holy, personal God of the Bible. It involved communication, thought, engagement, forbearance and humility – after all, you could be rejected, or worse! Yes, Satan was confronted, but neither directly, nor pompously. The orthodox view of spiritual warfare agrees that Satan does indeed blind people's minds to the truth, but not by holding spiritual hands over spiritual eyes! People are blinded to the Gospel through philosophies, ideologies, wrong assumptions and sinful patterns of thought. The spirit of this vanishing age will not be cast out of anybody, not to mention out of any city or locality. It must be challenged and deposed, one person at a time, with Truth!

But if our Gospel is hid, it is hidden to those who are lost, in whom the God of this world has blinded the minds of them which believe not, lest the light of the glorious gospel of Christ, who is the image of God, should shine unto them. (II Corinthians 4:3-4)

The new Gnostics have developed a more mystical and experiential approach to spiritual warfare. Through extra-biblical revelation, our new "generals" of the spirit, have discerned that we can "take our cities for God" by determining the name and characteristics of the ruling "territorial spirits" otherwise referred to frequently as "strong men". Once identified, these "strong men" can be focused on by believers through prayers, imprecations, curses, and symbolic actions (prayer marches, stake-driving ceremonies, war dances, pageants, repenting for sinful actions of the past, repenting on behalf of whole people groups), these "strong men" can be deposed, so that a whole city can come to God.

None of the above were ever practised by Jesus or the apostles, but that doesn't seem to faze many people these days. It seems to work, it feels good to be doing something, it is personally exalting and flattering to think that you are "warring" up in the highest levels of the spiritual realm. Those involved are convinced that by their practices, something effective is being done. There are many "spiritual warfare experts" who have become so adept at these practices, they can "map" whole cities, regions, and even nations, to determine the names of the ruling spirits over them!

This is just one current example of how Christianity is being redefined. It has been mysticised into something which neither Jesus nor the apostles ever practised. Faith which is Logos centred; the *"faith once and for all time delivered to the saints"*, has been replaced by mystical experience, pageants, marches, symbolic activity, vicarious acts of repentance, and even pilgrimages! The new Christianity is more akin to medieval Catholicism and even paganism, than it is to the spirituality of the early church. The thing to remember is that none of this is new. The church has always been plagued with attempts at redefining the knowledge of God. John spoke to the problem through the Holy Spirit and we would do well to consider his writing.

The Christians John writes to in his letter had been unsettled in their confidence. They were almost persuaded that really they didn't know anything, certainly not anything significant, of God! After all, they weren't "spiritual" like the Gnostics; they hadn't seen Jesus, nor had they had encounters with the different levels of angels. (They weren't even spiritual enough to receive the revelation that there were levels and hierarchies of angels!). These "super spiritual" apostles and prophets really knew God! They really had the "New Anointing"! And what was it that John's readers had? Not much really. They had the Scriptures. (Knowing God through a book? Head knowledge!) They also had the teachings of the apostles. (Can you imagine that? Following a mere man!) Finally, they had simple prayer; no trances, shaking, or altered states of consciousness, just plain-old, *"asking according to His will*, and *"believing on the name of Jesus"*, of course with the provision that *"we keep His commandments"* (I John 3:20-23).

These Christians had never seen Jesus, and were waiting for Him to return bodily, in the air, to complete their salvation. Compared to the claims of the Gnostics, this all seemed too simplistic and even carnal! Gnostics promoted the Platonic idea that matter was inherently evil. Therefore they denied the incarnation and spiritualised everything Jesus did or said. If they weren't tempted to become Gnostics, they were certainly shaken in their own knowledge of God, and considered it inadequate by comparison.

John's task is simple. It is to set straight who it is that really knows God and who doesn't. It is to know who truly is "anointed" and who isn't. What does it mean to know God anyway? I John spends a lot of time making these distinctions and telling true "garden variety" Christians what it is that "we know". His is no new message, but that which we received at the beginning.

*. . .Hereby we do know that we **know** Him, if we keep His commandments. He that saith I know Him and keepeth not His commandments is a liar and the truth is not in him". (I John 2:3-4)*

*But you have an unction from the Holy One and **know** all things, I have not written unto you because you know not the Truth but because you do **know** it, and that no lie is of the Truth. (I John 2:20-21.)*

14

Little children, let no man deceive you, he that doeth righteousness is righteous, even as He is righteous . . . He that committeth sin is of the Devil. (I John 3:7-8.)

We know that we are of God, and the whole world lies in wickedness. And we know that the Son of God has come and has given us an understanding, that we may know Him that is true, and we are in Him that is true, even in His Son Jesus Christ. This is the true God and eternal life. (I John 5:19-20.)

What John says to the fathers, young men and dear children of the Faith, in assuring them that it is they and not the Gnostics, who are the real "knowing ones", can be distilled down to three simple theological statements, which are helpful tests. These make up the essence of the genuine faith that truly "overcomes the world" and gives eternal life. They are as follows:

. . .God is Light . . . (I John 1:5.)
. . .God is love . . . (I John 4:8.)
. . .Jesus Christ has come [and remains: Greek] *in the flesh . . . (I John 4:2.)*

In these three statements John offers to all of us a badly needed repair of the nets, a salve for the torn and confused faith of those ravaged and disillusioned by the new 'super-spirituality', and its total reassignment of the definitions and applications of every basic tenet of Christianity.

Let us examine them individually.

CHAPTER I

GOD IS LIGHT

This then is the message we have heard of Him and declare we unto you, that God is light and in Him is no darkness at all. (I John 1:5.)

THE OPENNESS OF GOD

John has no new message, but that which we have heard from God at the start. Our first love must be restored, we must go back to the first truth we had heard, namely, God is light. There is no darkness in God, no esoteric mysteries, or occult hidden teachings for the elite, and no hidden meanings behind the sayings of Jesus or the apostles. There are no "Lost books of the Bible", nor any "secret Bible codes", for all is out in the open. This was the confession of Jesus at His trial before Pilate, as John records,

I spoke openly to the world, I ever taught in the synagogue and in the temple, where the Jews always resort; and in secret have I said nothing. (John 18:20.)

Satan has contradicted this truth ever since the Garden of Eden, for he has deceived man into thinking that God has been withholding the real truth. *"God knows"*, the serpent whispered, *"that in the day you eat of it, **your eyes shall be opened**, and ye shall be as gods, knowing good and evil."* In other words you need to be enlightened, let in on the secret teaching of godhood, and the revelation which most are unaware of, which will empower you individually! There has been a consistent drawing in the direction of the arcane. Those who attain to it are initiated into an elite company; a higher level of spirituality. This has been a strong pull in every false religion and it has intruded itself into Christianity from time immemorial.

It is into the face of this "pseudo-spirituality" that John holds forth the sincerity of God; *God is light.* There are no "hidden teachings" for all is out in the open; *in the light!* If the Gospel is hidden (and it is to many), it is hidden from the proud and self-sufficient, and from the insincere, for they have been blinded by their own pride and sinfulness. The god of this passing age also blinds men from the Gospel by their false philosophies, vain ways of thinking and worldly perspectives.

God is light. He has no secret doctrines, no double meanings, no elite inner circle. Those who are "of God" are sincere as well. They have no double meaning to their teachings. Their doctrines don't have to be worked in on unsuspecting congregations. I have received materials from people, such as the Seventh Day Adventists, promoting their aberrant doctrines, but without ever mentioning the name, "Seventh Day Adventist" on any of it! They dissemble because they know that people are cautious, having some idea about their failed prophecies and Judaisation. This couldn't possibly be "of God" for *God is light.*

All of those who are of the darkness; Jehovah's Witnesses, Mormons, Moonies and the whole range of cults dissemble. They hide their "deeper teachings" until they sense an opening in those whom they seek to seduce. They are not above lying about what they believe, because like Satan they have an "ends justifies the means" rationale. The Moonies have given it the name "Heavenly Deception". Lies are always a major mark of the Serpent. Jesus warned us of this in John 8:

He [satan] *was a murderer from the beginning, and abode not in the truth, because there is no truth in him. When he speaks a lie, he speaks of his own for he is a liar and the father of it* [the Lie]. *(John 8:44.)*

LIGHT AS HOLINESS

The confession, "God is Light" has ethical implications as well, for the worship of a holy God should result in a personally holy life. Those who hold to a wrong concept of God inevitably end up morally wrong in some area. This was especially true of the Gnostics.

If we say that we have fellowship with Him and walk in darkness, we lie and do not the truth: but if we walk in the light as He is in the light, we have fellowship with one another and the blood of Jesus Christ His Son cleanses us from all sin. (I John 1:6-7.)

The Gnostics were strongly influenced by Greek Philosophy, especially Platonism. They held to a strong dualism between flesh and spirit. The material world was supposedly created by an evil god, *Jahweh*, who also happened to be the god of the Old Testament. Therefore, all matter was considered evil. Jesus, according to the Gnostics, had come not to save us from sin, but from the ignorance which kept us trapped in the material world. Thus the secret teaching, the *gnosis* (knowledge), was salvation, but not from the guilt of sin. To them salvation was from bondage to the physical world which they regarded as evil. As a consequence of this belief the Gnostics also held that Jesus could not possibly have come, nor remain in the flesh. This we will look at in a later chapter.

This false dichotomy resulted in two equally pernicious errors; a harsh asceticism and a total licentiousness. Since they believed that Spirit was ideal and the highest good, then the goal of life would be to escape flesh, and to renounce as much of the material world as possible, in order to free oneself from the bonds of the physical body. One path into this was asceticism, in which salvation was realised through denial of physical appetites. You can see this played out in the example of the various monks and mystics who denied themselves such legitimate comforts as marriage, conjugal intimacy, foods, human companionship and even shelter! One outstanding example of this was a man who was considered a hero of the faith in the third century, one Simon Styletes. Simon the stylite was so named because he sat on a stylus (pillar) continuously for thirty-eight years!

This false dichotomy is more than just error, it is demonic!

Now the Spirit speaks expressly, that in the latter days, some shall depart from the Faith, giving heed to seducing spirits, and doctrines of demons, speaking lies in hypocrisy; having their conscience seared as with a hot iron; forbidding to marry and commanding to abstain from meats which God has created to be received with thanksgiving of them which believe and know the truth. (I Timothy 4:1-3.)

Another direction many would go in as a result of this artificial dualism between flesh and spirit was in outrageous licence. The thinking was that if it is only the spirit that matters, the body isn't significant. What you did in your body didn't matter for the physical world was supposedly not the real world. Flesh isn't real anyway, only spirit. Therefore, as long as you have the *gnosis*, or as long as you are "in Christ", you can do anything you desire physically. The only concept of sin is "ignorance". "In Christ" you are perfect and without sin regardless of what you do in the body! Only spirit counts, remember?

Thus you had Christianised Gnostics in churches who were homosexuals, fornicators, and practitioners of even worse perversions! It was to this kind of confusion that John spoke directly, calling us back to the basic theology that *"God is Light, and in Him there is no darkness at all"*, as well as these other statements:

If we say that we have no sin, we deceive ourselves and the truth is not in us, If we confess our sins, He is faithful and just to forgive us our sins and to cleanse us from all unrighteousness. If we say we have not sinned, we make him a liar and His word is not in us. (I John 1:8-10.)

Whosoever committeth sin transgresseth also the law; for sin is the transgression of the law. And ye know that he was manifested to take away our sins; and in Him there is no sin. Whoever abideth in Him sinneth not, whoever sinneth [habitually] hath not seen Him or known Him. Little children, let no man deceive you, He that doeth righteousness is righteous as He is righteousness, He that committeth sin is of the Devil, for the Devil sinned from the beginning. For this purpose the Son of God was manifested, that He might destroy the works of the Devil. (I John 3:4-8.)

Jesus Christ came to take away sin. Those who live or promote lawlessness *(iniquity)* have not known Him, regardless of the various revelations and mystical experiences. Those who are of God practice and advocate personal righteousness. This righteousness is an actual righteousness lived out in the real world. *"Let no man deceive you, he that doeth righteousness is righteous, even as He is righteous."* Righteousness is not merely a standing, it has concrete results. Those who are truly right with God will end up living right. Who you are spiritually and physically can't be divorced. God is holy.

Whosoever is born of God doth not commit sin, for His seed remaineth in Him, and he cannot sin because he is born of God. (I John 3:9)

Truly born again people cannot habitually and nonchalantly practice sin. Because His seed, the very Life that condemns sin, is in them, therefore they cannot practice sin. When they sin, they are convicted. A sign that you are really saved is the hatred of sin. To a mystical, Gnostic Christian, sin is no issue. Either they are ascetics seeking to escape the flesh, or they have exchanged the grace of God for lasciviousness, on the basis that all that really counts is the "spiritual you"; "who you are in Christ". Because *"God is light, and in Him is no darkness at all"*, the mark of a real believer is the abhorrence of all sin and iniquity.

THE LIGHT THAT REVEALS ALL

Finally, we are brought to the question, what is the function of light? Light reveals all things. To come to the true and living God, is to come *into the light*. This was one of the ways Jesus illustrated conversion in His conversation with Nicodemus.

And this is the condemnation, that light is come into the world, and men loved darkness more than the light, because their deeds were evil. For everyone that doeth evil hateth the light, lest His deeds should be reproved. But he that doeth truth cometh to the light, that his deeds should be made manifest that they are wrought in God. (John 3:19-21.)

What does it mean to *come to the light?* Coming into the light means coming out into the open, willing to be known before God for who you really are and what you have done. Reconciliation with God is reconciliation with Light and Truth. One day the whole world will be dragged into the light of God for *"there is nothing hidden that shall not be revealed"*. On the Judgment Day all will be seen for what it is. Every motive, action, word, thought and deed will be "out in the open", fully examined, and righteously judged. We who believe the true Gospel are not waiting for that day. We are coming to Him who is Light, voluntarily; He has *"called us out of darkness into His marvellous light"*!

The beauty of the light of God is that it not only exposes all, but it purges as well. There are two marvellous witnesses to this that come to mind; Peter and Isaiah.

In the year that King Uzziah died, I saw the Lord sitting on a throne, high and lifted up, and His train filled the temple. Above it stood the Seraphim, each one had six wings, with twain he covered his face, with twain he covered his feet and with twain did he fly. And one cried out to the other, Holy, Holy, Holy, is the Lord of Hosts, the whole earth is full of His glory! And the posts of the door moved at the voice of him that cried, and the whole house was filled with smoke. Then said I, Woe is me for I am undone; because I am a man of unclean lips and I dwell among a people of unclean lips; for my eyes have seen the King, the Lord of Hosts! (Isaiah 6:1-5.)

To Isaiah, an encounter with the true and living God of the Bible also included a dreadful self-revelation. He saw himself more clearly than he had ever seen himself before. Isaiah had been no ruffian or worthless fellow up to that time. He was a priest of the holy God, and lived a separated life devoted to the worship of God. The God of the Bible is never reluctant to reveal the flaws of His servants – David's adultery, and Abraham's lies – but we read of nothing incriminating to Isaiah in comparison to other men. However, in the light of God, Isaiah could see himself as the infinitely holy God could see him and that one glimpse slew Him! *"Woe is me! I am undone! I am a man of unclean lips and I dwell among a people of unclean lips, for my eyes have seen the King . . . !"*

Remember that John's purpose is to "repair our nets" and to call us back to the true God and eternal life. Any spirituality that is introduced in the name of Jesus Christ that lacks this element, of the penetrating light of God leading to self-abhorrence, is counterfeit, regardless of whatever mystical experiences it presents.

Was Isaiah really that bad? As I stated earlier, in comparison to other men, he lived a life separated to God. However, we will not be judged in comparison to other men. The standard is true holiness, Jesus Christ. In the very presence of his God, Isaiah could see his own truly profound sinfulness. Unclean lips? One television preacher posited that perhaps Isaiah had a "cursing spirit". He missed the point. Isaiah didn't have a cursing spirit, but was already by this time a preacher of righteousness. The best things he had ever said, in the light of God's holiness, were as curses. As Isaiah would say in a later sermon,

we are all as an unclean thing, and all of our righteousness are as filthy rags . . .
(Isaiah 64:6.)

The Gnostics and the super-spiritual were proclaiming their encounters with God, but had none of the brokenness and self-revulsion that a real encounter with God brings. In fact they were even making the claims that they had never sinned or were without sin!

Isaiah found out something else that is vital to true religion on that day when he was so undone in the sanctuary of God. If you are willing to stay in the light, no matter how uncomfortable, that same light exposes and purges. While he was standing in the light of the infinitely holy, personal God, trembling at the revelation of His own sinfulness, I have no doubt that Isaiah felt the impulse to run out of there with every fibre of his being. But fortunately, Isaiah stayed *in the light*. The text in Isaiah continues,

Then flew one of the Seraphim unto me, having a live coal in his hand, which he had taken with tongs from off of the altar. And he laid it upon my mouth and said, lo, this hath touched thy lips, and thine iniquity is taken away and thy sin purged. (Isaiah 6:6-7.)

Isaiah couldn't purge himself. He could only stand there renouncing himself before God, then allow God to purge him of his deep sinfulness, *"Lo, this hath touched thy lips..",. "If you confess with your mouth the Lord Jesus . . ."* There is no self-salvation, no ladder of ascent, only a coming into the light of God,

Neither is there any creature that is not manifest in His sight: but all things are naked and opened unto the eyes of Him with whom we have to do. (Hebrews 4:13.)

SIMON PETER COMES INTO THE LIGHT

And He entered into one of the ships, which was Simon's and prayed Him that he would thrust out a little from the land. And he sat down and taught the people out of the ship. Now when He had left off speaking, He said unto Simon, 'Launch out into the deep and let down your nets for a draught. And Simon answering said unto Him Master, we have toiled all the night, and have taken nothing; nevertheless at thy word I will let down the net, and when they had done this, they had enclosed a great multitude of fishes and their nets brake . . . When Simon Peter saw it he fell down at Jesus' knees saying, Depart from me for I am a sinful man, O Lord. (Luke 5:1-8.)

Here we have another illustration, one which John himself no doubt witnessed first hand, of a man encountering God, and thus his own fallenness. *"Depart from me, for I am a sinful man, O Lord!"* This was Peter's conversion. Once again, he stays in the light, that the true light might not only expose him, but purge him as well.

. . .And Jesus said unto Simon, Fear not, from now on you shall catch men. (Luke 5:10)

Coming to God is coming into the light of exposure. This light is every bit as uncomfortable as that which Isaiah and Peter found themselves standing in. A true encounter with the God of the Bible does not leave one "at peace with one's self", but rather renouncing one's self! The light is reality, it calls for humility and confession. Its fruit is a death to self justification and a humble and contrite vindication of God! The very thing many dread is the best thing that could ever happen, because the same light that exposes, purges us of that which is exposed.

If we confess our sins, He is faithful and just to forgive us our sins and to cleanse us from all unrighteousness. (I John 1:9.)

But if we walk in the light as He is in the light, we have fellowship with one another, and the blood of Jesus Christ His Son cleanses us from all sins. (I John 1:7.)

Sinners and the unrepentant hate and fear the light of God. They especially hate the idea that God sees all. To those who live a life that is in flight from God, it is unbearable to imagine that their whole life is under the scrutiny of God. Judgment Day is a summons, a subpoena into the Light. To stand before God, naked and ashamed, is probably worse than the lake of fire itself. Perhaps it will be a sort of relief to actually be escorted back out of the light of God's holy face, and into the sentence reserved for darkness! The real God is light and in Him is no darkness at all!

In summary, because God is light, there are no secret teachings for the elite "super Christians". God is open and sincere. The "hidden things of darkness" belong to the occult and are the mark of satanic religion and not of the holy, sincere and personal God of the Bible. Furthermore those who are of God make no artificial distinctions between "spiritual righteousness" and living lives that seek to be pleasing to God. We know that those who don't habitually practice righteousness are not of God but of the Devil, regardless of their boasted "spirituality". Whoever is really of God hates sin, and knows that sin is not "ignorance" it is the breaking of God's law. Lawless spirituality is not Christian. Finally, a real encounter with God will lead to a self-exposure that slays confidence in the flesh and selfishness: *"I am undone!"* and *"Depart from me, I am a sinful man, O Lord!"* That is what real apostles and prophets confessed. God is light, light exposes sin and iniquity, and those who have encountered the real God hate sin and iniquity. In the end, at the Judgment Day, those who have covered themselves will be brought out into the light and they will be uncovered. Those who, because of the Gospel, have uncovered themselves, and have come out into the light, will discover that the same light that reveals all things also purges. *"God is light"* is the first of three statements John makes in his restoration of our souls back to *"That which is true."*

CHAPTER 2

GOD IS LOVE

And we have known and believed the love God has to us, God is love; and he that dwelleth in love dwelleth in God, and God in Him. (I John 4:16.)

In calling us back to genuine Christianity, to *"that which is from the beginning"*, John makes a second simple but profound theological statement: *God is Love.* Love is the mark of the "only true God". Those who have known Him will walk in love. Those who hate or who consistently fail to love the brethren, reveal that they do not truly know Him, regardless of their supposed spirituality.

Brethren, I write no new commandment unto you, but an old commandment which ye had from the beginning. The old commandment is the Word which ye had at the beginning. Again, a new commandment I write unto you, which thing is true in Him and in you: because the darkness is past, and the true light now shineth. He that saith He is in the light and hateth his brother is in darkness even until now. He that loveth his brother abideth in the light and there is none occasion of stumbling in him. (I John 2:7-10.)

Those who claim to "know God" and to be in the light, contradict those very claims when they live loveless, uncharitable, and even self seeking lives. Agape love is the mark of the Christian, for *"God is love"*. The mission of Jesus was a mission of love also. Those who have seen Jesus, and through Him have known God, are people who love.

On the other hand, Gnosticism, and artificial Christianity, is all about self. The quest is to come into the secret knowledge of "who you are in Christ" (the essence of that secret being in one form or another that the self is divine – Satan's original lie). The whole thrust of modern artificial Christianity is really all about self-discovery or some kind of self fulfilment and healing. What are the followers of the Toronto Blessing or the Pensacola "River" chartering buses for? Nothing more than a personal blessing and an experience to enrich the self. In spite of the fact that God has given us the more sure word of prophecy, they seek some kind of a personal "word" from a Rick Joyner or a Bill Hamon. They long to be part of the elite company (sometimes called "manchild" company) rather than just being willing to take their place among the redeemed of the ages. They long to be known as the "cutting edge", great endtime army, which all of the church through the ages has looked for!

Part of the deception is that there is so much lip service given to the idea of "love". Everybody acknowledges love these days; love for God, love for one another, love for those who have failed, and love expressed in a strong passion to "tear down the denominational walls that separate the body". In this sense, we have never lived in such loving times.

What does it mean to love God? How does one know that he really loves God? There is much confusion on this subject in these sensual, religious times. To many, the answer to the question, "Do you love God?", requires a simple answer that can be answered without any hesitation, "Of course I love God! I am wild about God; I can't wait to get my next experience of Him, I get loaded on God; I love God so much I am addicted to being in His 'presence'." How do you know if you love God? There is a whole generation of "revival Christians" whose answer to that would be something along the lines of, "I've been so caught up in God, I got drunk in the spirit, I have been 'laid out' for four hours or more, caught up in the Glory; God hit me so hard I couldn't stop shaking for hours and even days. How could you question my love for God?"

To these sensualised Christians, we are dead, dry, sucking on prunes, or worse yet, "religious"! We don't have anything they would want, for they have been conditioned to think that knowing and loving God is a sensual experience, and in a good many cases even an erotic experience. Having to rely on the Bible, preaching, doctrine, waiting for the actual return of the Lord, witnessing, praying and awaiting with patient suffering the answer to prayers, strikes these false converts as being "religious and dead". In our services, we don't get 'zapped' nor do we stagger about the sanctuary, drunk in the spirit. Thus they conclude that we lack "passion for Jesus", whereas they in their constant seeking of "the presence" – the "glory" which overcame John Kilpatrick to the point that he had to be helped into his clothes every morning for weeks – they have their passion.

THE CONTEXT FOR LOVE

This is love alright, but it is not *Agape*. It is *Eros*. This is one of the major confusing aspects of the current false revival. When I went to Toronto to research my book *Weighed and Found Wanting; Putting the Toronto Blessing in Context*, I spent quite a bit of time at the Toronto Airport Vineyard, sitting through services, interviewing people and just watching. Part of the atmosphere in the services touched a place in my heart, particularly the worship. I had been involved in the Charismatic renewal twenty years ago, and the worship in Toronto seemed to be a throwback to those days. The songs were of love and devotion to Jesus and the Holy Spirit. The scene in the congregation was one of young and old, rough looking youths, distinguished looking adults, church kids, street kids, and people of all walks of life lifting up hands to God in worship and love. Seemingly, isn't this is what we all want? People of all walks of life united in praising and worshipping God! But they proceeded from that into blatant spiritual hedonism! After all, who does anybody ever get drunk for? Has anybody ever gotten drunk for anyone other then themselves? It looked like love, felt and sounded like love. Yet it was a different kind of love: Eros; a love for the sake of mutual gratification. Loving the religious feeling, the abandonment, the idea of being one of the super-spiritual elite. Perhaps they loved the power to slay or be slain in the spirit, or splashing the waters of the 'river' on each other. They certainly imagined that such displays brought pleasure to God. Of course that is not what the apostles meant when they admonished us to love God, nor when they told us that *God is love.*

How does one know if he truly loves God? There is a context for loving God, for Jesus said,

If ye love me, keep my commandments. (John 14:15.)

The context of loving God is not mere ecstasy, but it is Light. *"God is light and in Him there is no darkness at all . . . God is Love."* I must admit that I am all for feeling my religion from time to time. After twenty years, I still believe in "lifting holy hands to Him", and that he touches us, and allows us even to feel His holy presence. He heals and delivers and answers prayer. Though these are all wonderful and valid blessings, none of these is the measure or context for gauging love. If we love God, we believe in His Son and keep His commandments.

There is in modern popular Christianity an artificial wall of separation between love and law. The apostles knew no such distinction. To love God is to want to obey Him. Lawlessness is the very opposite of love.

It could be that we have adopted this false concept as a reaction to legalistic religion. Wanting to obey God's word is not legalism. True love wants to obey God, not grudgingly as a means to attain salvation, but because He has loved us and saved us, we want to treat God and others righteously. Love and obedience are linked in the thought of Jesus and the apostles. Law is not the means of my salvation, but it is the measure of my love for God and others. Salvation could only come through the death of Jesus Christ, and not by works.

Whosoever believeth that Jesus is the Christ is Born of God: and everyone that loveth him that begat, loveth him also that is begotten of Him. By this we know that we love the children of God, when we love God and keep His commandments. For this is the love of God, that we keep his commandments, and his commandments are not grievous. (I John 5:1-3.)

AGAPE AS A RESPONSE TO AGAPE

. . .love is of God . . . Herein is love, not that we loved God, but that he loved us . . . We love him because he first loved us. (I John 4:7, 10, 19.)

The love that is genuine, Agape, does not come from us. It is initiated by God. We didn't decide to discover God one day, He had to reveal Himself to us. He sought us and bought us, as the old song proclaims. He did something about our desperate situation when we were helpless and yet in our sin. God has loved us as an act of free, undeserved grace. All we can ever do is respond to that love in faith and in love. *"We love him, because he first loved us . . ."* (I John 4:19.) Why did God love us? What did He see in us? Nothing lovable at all. He loved us because He chose to love us. And how do we know God loves us?

In this was manifested the love of God toward us, because that God sent His only Begotten Son into the world that we might live through Him. (I John 4:9.)

31

But God commendeth His love toward us, in that while we were yet sinners, Christ died for us. (Romans 5:8.)

The evidence of the love of God is both subjective and objective. How do we know that God loves us? On the objective side, God has taken an initiative in order to save us. The incarnation, death and resurrection of Jesus is the proof of the love of God. To doubt that God loves you, or to insist on a sign of that love is unbelief of the highest order. Much of the basis for the current expression of sensual Christianity is that God is supposedly trying to show His people that he loves them. God has shown us conclusively that He loves us when He invaded time and space to save us!

And we have known and believed the love that God hath to us . . . (I John 4:16.)

The subjective evidence is the giving of the Spirit and our adoption as sons. *"In the fullness of time, God sent forth His son . . . and because ye are sons, God has sent forth the spirit of His son, crying Abba, Father" (Galatians 4:4,6).* The Spirit of adoption which we have received sends out a cry within the hearts of all true Christians. The heart cry to the God and Father of our Lord Jesus Christ is *"Abba, Father!"* This witness of the Holy Spirit, this inner conviction against sin, this heart-cry to God the Father, this inner witness to the truth and testimony against error, is the subjective witness to the love of God.

Behold what manner of love the Father has given unto us, that we should be called the sons of God . . . And this is His commandment, that we should believe on the name of His Son Jesus Christ, and love one another, as he gave us commandment. And he that keepeth His commandments, dwelleth in Him and He in him. And hereby we know that He abideth in us, by the Spirit He hath given us. (I John 3:1, 23-24.)

32

NOT AS CAIN

Those who have known this love through belief and acceptance of the Gospel, will love. As God has freely forgiven us, we have no choice, we forgive those who sin against us. Love is so basic to Christianity, whoever doesn't have it, has every reason to totally doubt their salvation.

We know that we have passed from death unto life, because we love the brethren. He that loveth not his brother abideth in death. (I John 3:14.)

Cain and Abel were both worshippers. They both professed by their actions that they loved God. Abel came to God through the revelation of God (through the Word) bringing the bloody sacrifice. He came unto God on God's terms (by God's law) thus proving his love for God. Cain was a Gnostic, he would not be as common worshippers, "stuck on the Bible", worshipping according to the revealed way. He had his own revelation, a higher approach. He came to God on his own terms. He loved God *his* way. When he was rejected by God, he hated his brother for being and doing right, thus proving that he never really loved God or his brother.

For this is the message that ye have heard from the beginning, that we should love one another. Not as Cain, who was of that wicked one and slew his brother. And wherefore slew he him? Because his own works were evil and his brother's righteous.
(I John 3: 11-12.)

Cain is an everlasting sign that not all that is religious is truly spiritual and not all love for God is really love for God. He was a worshipper, but an innovator; a Gnostic operating in his own revelation of how God ought to be worshipped. He would have argued that he loved God, perhaps even in a higher and more advanced way than his

33

unsophisticated brother. When it became evident that God rejected his self-willed sacrifice, that kind of love revealed itself to be hatred and even murder! Cain had love, religious impulses and passion, and he wanted the presence of God, but it was love out of context, lawless love, love on his own terms.

THE LOVE THAT LAYS ITS LIFE DOWN

Herein is love, not that we loved God, but that he loved us, and sent His Son to be the propitiation for our sins. Beloved, if God so loved us, we ought also to love one another. (I John 4:10-11.)

Hereby perceive we the love of God, because He laid down His life for us; and we ought to lay our lives down for the brethren. But whoso hath this world's good and seeth his brother have need' and shutteth up his bowels of compassion from him, how dwelleth the love of God in him? My little children, let us not love in word, neither in tongue; but in deed and in truth. (I John 3:16-18.)

Note that the example John shows points to the fact that love is a concrete practical reality. Love is a choice. It is not a spiritualised feeling. In fact it is giving and seeking the other's good, even to our own expense. We don't often have the chance to lay down our lives in the ultimate sense as Jesus did when He died for us. The love of God will compel us to lay down our own concerns, priorities, and self-seeking in countless small ways, for example when the need of a brother comes before us. To not have compassion and willingness to share and give of ourselves in the little things is evidence of spiritual death.

This is not to say that all Christians are perfectly mature in their love. Love grows in our lives. It starts with the Gospel, the realisation that God has loved me, a sinner! He has taken a costly step to save me. When I was His enemy, He sent His Son. Having received Jesus, I am now adopted into the family of God (incredible!). This love is my belief. It is transforming me, and the way I see everything. Who am I not to love others and not to forgive any? There will be ample opportunities to grow in this love for offences will come and people will hurt us. Will we choose to love anyway? When we are maligned, and despitefully used, what will our response be? John speaks of a perfect love, a matured love which casts out fear.

There is no fear in love; but perfect love casteth out fear because fear hath torment. He that feareth is not made perfect in love. (I John 4:18.)

What is it about love that casts out fear? Fear can be summed up in one question, "What about me?" Fear asks, in every situation, "What is going to happen to me?" God has loved us, taken care of us, and done something about our sinful situation we could never do ourselves; He has redeemed us. Do you believe this? If so, how do you react to this? Whoever truly believes the good news, loves as a response. No longer is my question, "What about me?" I am free now from my concern because I have been and will be taken care of. I can now ask, "What about you?" In this way, perfect love casts out fear and particularly the fear of Judgment Day. Jesus came and gave, He loved people every day of His life, and even when they mocked Him, and murdered Him he prayed for them. Those who follow Him love also. Therefore they aren't afraid of judgment. Those who love have confidence;

Herein is our love made perfect, that we may have boldness in the day of judgment: because as He is, so are we in this world. (I John 4:17.)

Those who refuse to love have no assurance of salvation. Those who love as they have been loved by Him are confident even in the Day of Judgment. The world cannot see God, but if we love one another they will see Him. None of this is complicated, because this is no new message. Christianity is love; if there is no love, there is no Christianity. It is a love in context, in other words it is the love that shows itself in obedience to God, not like Cain's love which became hatred. It is the love which is revealed in the Light. The two don't contradict, they go together; *God is Love . . . God is Light.* God is all merciful, and at the same time He is fearful in holiness! How do these come together? How can God be the loving Saviour and the holy Judge in one at the same time? These two attributes are met together and they are embodied in the simple statement, *"Jesus Christ came in the flesh."*

CHAPTER 3

JESUS CHRIST CAME IN THE FLESH

Hereby know ye the Spirit of God; Every spirit that confesseth that Jesus Christ is come in the flesh is of God; every spirit that confesseth not that Jesus Christ is come in the flesh is not of God; and this is that spirit of anti-christ, whereof you have heard that it should come. (I John 4:2-3.)

We have thus far examined two of the three propositions that John has given us in order to help us to discern that faith *"which is from the beginning"*, regarding true Christianity. There is the test of light, the test of love, and finally a test of truth, particularly the truth concerning the person of Christ. *"Jesus Christ has come* [and remains] *in the flesh."*

For many deceivers are entered into the world, who confess not that Jesus Christ is come in the flesh. This is the deceiver and an anti-christ. Look to yourselves, that we lose not those things which we have wrought, but that we receive a full reward. Whosoever transgresseth and abideth not in the doctrine of Christ, hath not God. He that abideth in the doctrine of Christ hath both the Father and the Son. (2 John 7-9.)

Is doctrine important? John thinks so. The doctrine of Christ is so important that to leave it is called a transgression, and whoever will not remain in it no longer has God! Far from de-emphasising doctrine, seeking to distil it to the lowest common denominator, the apostles insisted on the importance of doctrine, particularly this doctrine concerning the person of Christ.

What is this doctrine? The heart of it is that the man Jesus Christ is God. He has come and remains in the flesh, that He might be our redeemer. Though He was, is and always will be God, He remains a man, He is the *monogenes* – the only begotten (unique) Son of God. There is no one like Him, God and man in one and the same person. In some way, Satan, through the Spirit of anti-christ will seek to deny this doctrine, for reasons which we will state later. Suffice it to say that if Satan can spiritualise Christ, he can more easily counterfeit Him.

DOCETISM

The ancient Gnostics held to the Platonic notion (as stated earlier) that the physical realm is actually an aberration, an evil distortion of the ideal realm, which is the realm of the Spirit. Anything physical was held to be a corruption, or at best a mere shadow of the Ideal. Salvation meant escape from physical bondage, and the body was seen as the prison house of the soul. If the Jews were offended by the *skandalon* of the cross, the Greeks were scandalised by something far more basic: the Incarnation. How could a God become a mere man? Why would a God come in the flesh? How could the *Logos* come in the flesh and dwell among us? There were only two options available to Platonically influenced Greeks who were touched by the Gospel message; either humble oneself, letting go of Greek philosophical presuppositions and embracing the message of the (Jewish) apostles, or modify and reinterpret Christianity to satisfy the Platonic thinking of more modern and sophisticated minds. By John's day, many Hellenistic converts were wholeheartedly doing the latter.

This produced several distortions mainly centred around the person of Christ. One early example was *Docetism*. This name is derived from the Greek word *dokein*, which means to seem, or to appear. The error was in the assertion that Jesus only *seemed* to be in the flesh, and He only *appeared* to suffer and die on the cross. Jesus was completely spiritual, so

38

spiritual that one early Gnostic claimed that when he walked through the sand he left no footprints! Another aspect of it was that instead of going to the cross (how could you crucify a spirit?), Jesus substituted Judas in his place and watched the crucifixion from a distance, laughing. This brand of Docetism evidently was what Mohammed was exposed to as a youth, therefore the Qu'ran passes this off as an account of the cross. Salvador Dali's painting of the last supper has a Docetic Christ. On close inspection, one can see the landscape through Christ, for Dali's version of Christ is transparent!

Note the concrete physicality in the descriptions of Jesus by the apostles:

That which was from the beginning, which we have heard, which we have seen with our eyes, which we have looked upon, and our hands have handled, of the Word of Life. (I John 1:1.)

And the Word was made flesh, and dwelt among us . . . (John 1:14.)

Him God raised up the third day, and shewed Him openly: not to all the people, but unto witnesses chosen before of God, even to us who did eat and drink with Him, after He rose from the dead. (Acts 10:40-41.)

They ate with Him. He fell asleep in the back of the boat. He prayed with *"loud crying and tears." (Hebrews 5:7.)* He cried, shouted, wept, and suffered. There was no doubt in the disciples' minds that the man they lived with, worked with, walked, talked, ate and slept with, was no ghost. *"Jesus Christ has come* [and remains] *in the flesh!"* The accounts of the death and resurrection are so vividly physical. The cross would have given you splinters had you run your hand up it; the nails, the flogging, the crown of thorns, the stone tomb, and the great stone blocking the way (which would have broken your foot had it rolled over it!) all being physical, point to Jesus' incarnation. The swaddling clothes that they wrapped him in; the tomb of the Sanhedrinist, Joseph of Arimethea; the certification of His death by Pilate; the sword piercing the side pouring out water and blood; the Roman seal over the mouth of the tomb, are in the Bible described in an entirely physical and concrete manner. This was no spiritualised account of auras, vibrations, unintelligible messages, it's all so flesh and blood! Locked in time and space, *"on the third day, they took him down from the tree and laid him in a sepulchre" (Acts 13:29).*

The accounts of the resurrection and its aftermath are particularly unspiritualised. Four times we are told that Jesus ate with people. *"John and Peter ran down to the site of the tomb, John got there first, but entered not."* Peter lumbering along, ducked his head and entered the tomb. They both saw something very physical that made them believe: the undisturbed grave clothes that had received 100lbs of embalming spices, but empty of the body of Jesus. Jesus made the apostles breakfast, made them count out the 153 fish he helped them to catch. Thomas handled the scars in his side and hands. This was no spiritualised death and resurrection.

Paul brought this out in his battle with incipient Gnosticism which had arisen among his Greek congregation, the Corinthians. Their problem was that they denied the bodily resurrection.

For I deliver unto you first of all . . . that Christ died for our sins according to the scriptures, and that He was buried and that He rose again the third day according to the scriptures: and that He was seen of Cephas, then of the twelve. (I Corinthians 15:3-5.)

How do we know he died? He was buried, embalmed, encased in burial clothes, and laid within a tomb. How do we know he arose? He was seen by Peter, the Twelve, His brother James (who really didn't believe in Him until that point), and later by 500 people at once.

WE NEED THOSE SCARS

The point is, Docetism is of the anti-christ. The denial that Jesus came in the flesh robs the church of the comfort of shared suffering with Christ. How comforting would it be to have a saviour who never really lived the human life, who never tasted suffering, pain, disappointment, or shame? It might appeal to those who, like the so-called Christian Science cults, seek to escape the harsh realities of this fallen world by denying the validity of pain and sorrow. This approach is demonic and merciless. The Gospel gives us a Saviour who fully entered into our condition, has experienced the human dilemma entirely, and out of whose sufferings relief and healing has come to countless sufferers down through time.

An English poet, Edward Shillito, writing after World War I, compared our wounded, pierced God to the remote and seemingly all powerful and impassive idols man seems to construct:

The other Gods were strong;
But Thou wast weak;
They rode, but Thou didst stumble to a throne;
But to our wounds only God's wounds can speak,
And not a God has wounds, but Thou alone.

Another current manifestation of Docetism is in the false prosperity gospel, which teaches, in true Gnostic form, that any kind of suffering is a result of ignorance of "revelation knowledge". This is cruelty to suggest that if one isn't healed, or wealthy, one is lacking faith.

ADOPTIONISM: THE FALSE ANOINTING

Another attempt to reconcile the doctrine of Christ with Greek categories of thinking was Adoptionism. This was the belief that Jesus was nothing more than a man until He was anointed by the Holy Ghost, which made Him a kind of a demi-god, a divine human being, by the anointing. The anointing supposedly came upon Him at the waters of the Jordan, and lifted from Him when He went to the cross. Therefore it could be said, that the man Jesus suffered, but God never suffered. What Jesus did in His life was solely through the anointing. Therefore, if you receive the same anointing, you can do the same thing! Kenneth Copeland goes so far as to say that God showed Him he could have died on the cross to redeem us if he had the same "revelation knowledge" as Jesus!

John speaks directly against this belief when he states that Jesus was, is and always has been the Son of God, the Christ. There was never a time that he *became* the Christ, nor a time when He wasn't the Christ. He is the same yesterday, today, and forever.

Who is he that overcometh the world, but he that believeth that Jesus is the Son of God? This is he that came by water and blood, even Jesus Christ; not by water only, but by water and blood. (I John 5:5-6.)

In other words, Jesus didn't become the Christ when He went into the river Jordan, to be baptised, and the Holy Ghost came upon Him. He came into that water as the Christ of God. Nor did He cease being the Christ when He began to pour out His precious blood for our redemption. There can never be a distinction between Jesus and Christ.

Jesus is the anointed of God, the Christ! Christ is not a state of being, nor is it (Christhood) the attainment of a certain few, but Christ is a person who is God and who came in the flesh. He became a man, died on the cross and arose from the dead! He came by water and blood, and ironically water and blood poured out of His heart when He was pierced, as a testimony of His physical death.

Otherwise Kenneth Copeland is right, Jesus is no different than any other "born again" man! You too can receive a special anointing . . . you can be a Christ also! (The word Christ means "anointed one".) Have you heard of the Toronto anointing, the Pensacola anointing, the Benny Hinn anointing, or Rodney Howard Browne's new anointing? These people introducing new anointings, are in effect introducing new Christs. People will charter buses and make pilgrimages just to partake of the latest dose of the new anointing, not realising that they are literally fulfilling scriptural warnings such as Matthew 24:23-24,

Then if any man shall say to you, Lo, here is Christ, or there; believe it not. For false Christs will arise, and false prophets, and shall show great signs and wonders; so that, if it were possible, they would deceive the very elect.

They aren't saying they are seeing Jesus in the flesh in Pensacola or Toronto. What is it they are saying is happening? A new anointing (Christ) is being poured out. "Increasing the anointing", "walking in the new apostolic anointing", "the prophetic anointing", or even the "end time anointing" are names given to countless seminars advertised in *Charisma* magazine and other Charismatic and Pentecostal outlets. Everybody is talking in terms of the anointing. How timeless is John's warning to us not to be impressed by "new anointings":

But ye have an unction from the Holy One and ye know all things . . . But the anointing which ye have received of Him abideth in you, and ye need not that any man should teach you, but as the same anointing teacheth you of all things, and is truth, and is no lie, and even as it hath taught you, ye shall abide in Him. (I John 2:20,27.)

John doesn't deny that Christians have an anointing, but the concept is different than the one currently taught. Rather than being something special, for an elite few, John holds that every believer has an anointing, because Christ is anointed, therefore we all have a share of Christ. This anointing, which all true believers have, is an anointing to know things, an inner witness to truth. We need no Gurus. Don't let anyone impress you with the idea that they have a special anointing. All Christians have an anointing to know the truth; stick with this anointing.

The error of adoptionism is that it separates Jesus from Christ. Christ is an anointing that came upon Jesus and it can come upon you as well if you will receive the secret knowledge or submit to the new apostle. This is a lie! Jesus is, was and always will be *the* Christ. From all eternity, through the waters of his baptism, even in his blood shedding on the cross, and at the right hand of the Father, Jesus is the Christ, the only Anointed One of God. Any anointing we have is our share of Him common to all believers. In the next section we will explore why it is that the Anti-christ seeks to deny this.

CHAPTER 4

THE ASSURANCE

Whatsoever is born of God overcometh the World, and this is the victory that overcometh the world, even our faith . . . (I John 5:4.)

That which we have seen and heard declare we unto you, that you also may have fellowship with us; and truly our fellowship is with the Father and with His Son, Jesus Christ. And these things write we unto you, that your joy may be full. (I John 1:3-4.)

Who really knows God? How do we know that we know Him? One of the dangers of false spirituality is the confusion it engenders, among the people of God. I spent five years caught up in the Word of Faith movement of Kenneth Hagin and Kenneth Copeland. When I was first exposed to these men and their teachings, I had to question my own spirituality. Jesus appeared to these men in dreams and visions, He interrupted their sermons to speak to them. Why didn't these things ever happen to me? All I seemed to have was justification by faith, the hope of heaven and the bible. Was I saved? Did I ever really know God?

Five years later, upon the realisation that these men and the movement spawned by their teachings was heretical, I found myself in another spiritual crisis. Once again I had to ask myself, "What else do I believe that is heretical? Have I been saved? Is what I had always believed I had experienced of the Holy Spirit valid? Do I really know God? I was off when I was in the Faith movement, what makes me think I am not totally off?" These experiences are extremely painful and more common than many realise. Like the Fathers, Little Children and Young Men John wrote to, I needed clarification, I needed assurance. Who is it that knows God? How do I know that I am even saved? What are the distinguishing marks of saving faith?

This beloved apostle, the one who leaned on Jesus' breast at the last supper, offers us five characteristics that mark true Christianity. Remember that he writes to us that we may enter into the fellowship of the Father and His Son and that our joy may be full. Peace and joy are gone when we are robbed of the assurance of salvation. We can examine ourselves in the light of these and "see if we be in the faith".

TRUE CHRISTIANS JUSTIFY GOD

If we say that we have fellowship with Him, and walk in darkness, we lie and do not the truth; if we walk in the light as He is in the light we have fellowship with one another, and the blood of Jesus Christ His Son cleanses us from all sin. If we say that we have no sin, we deceive ourselves and the truth is not in us. If we confess our sins, He is faithful and just to forgive us our sins, and to cleanse us from all unrighteousness. If we say that we have not sinned, we make him a liar, and his word is not in us. (I John 1:6-10.)

Those who really have known Him are marked not by whether or not they have had experiences of a mystical sort, but rather by whether they have ever been brought by the truth of God's Word to renounce their excuses, rationalisations and other forms of self-justification, and have simply justified God. This is what Paul meant when he proclaimed that the work of God's law was to bring people to the point when, *"Every mouth will be stopped and all the world will become guilty before God." (Romans 3:19).*

46

The problem lies in the fact that in order to justify God one must condemn oneself. This the sinner is unwilling to do. Sinners justify themselves and in the process condemn God. Condemning God is the inevitable result of self-justification. *"If we say that we have not sinned, we make Him a liar . . ."* people talk about miracles, signs and wonders, but the greatest miracle is when a sinner is brought to the point of dropping all excuses and just coming around to admitting, "God you are right!"

This issue of justifying God is huge. He feels strongly about it, it is no small matter. In fact, by the time of the end, *"every knee will bow, and every tongue shall confess that Jesus Christ is Lord."* Ultimately everyone will justify God, all will finally acknowledge, *"Just and true are your ways, thou King of the Saints, who wouldn't fear you and glorify your name?"* Every soul, in heaven, and on earth and even in Hell will all be brought to the point where they justify God. This is not to say that all will be saved, however. Rather I am saying that by the time Jesus is through, there will no longer be even a pocket of rebellion, no shaking fists, no longer any accusations against the Love or the Holiness of God. Even in Hell, the Hitlers and Mussolinis and Judases and Elvises will all have to admit that God is right, that He is good, that they deserve their fate, and that God has been holy and loving in all of His ways. Justifying God simply means admitting that God is right.

And all the people that heard him, and the publicans, justified God being baptised with the baptism of John, but the Pharisees and lawyers rejected the council of God against themselves, being not baptised by Him. (Luke 7:29-30.)

When John the Baptist brought the message of God to the people, it was far from flattering. The law of God condemned them as fallen, and under judgment. The common people heard John out, admitted that his preaching was right and justified God. The Pharisees refused to admit God's condemnation of themselves, they rejected the council of God against themselves. They justified themselves and condemned God (without realising it).

Thus it is today, although often it is hidden. Rarely will a person come out and say "I am without sin", although that is the prevailing view of our times. Psychology is the major Phariseeism of our times, shielding people from the demands and condemnations of the law of God by redefining sin, stripping away the moral responsibility of it, making void the Word of God. The Word of God declares that *"the unrighteous shall not inherit the kingdom of God . . . neither fornicators, nor idolaters, nor adulterers, nor effeminate, nor abusers of themselves with mankind, nor thieves, nor covetous, nor drunkards . . . shall inherit the Kingdom of God."* Well there you have it, that is what God says. Is He right?

Christian Psychology says, "Wait just one minute! You may have a drinking problem, you may even be an alcoholic, but who is to say that you aren't also a Christian, after all Christians all have problems too." In other words, I have no sin, I have a condition, a disease I inherited from my family. I was raised in a disfunctional home. One man told me, after being put out of the church for adultery, "You don't understand, I'm not a fornicator, I am a sex addict!" Through exchanging the condemning names for these sins, that God assigned to them, for more clinical names, we in effect say "You have no sin." God talks about sins, we talk about conditions.

You can tell the true and false Christians in this psychologised age. The true ones will always justify God, the false ones will justify themselves.

God forbid, let God be true and every man a liar, as it is written, that Thou mightest be justified when thou speakest and mightest overcome when Thou art judged. (Romans 3:4.)

Did the woman caught in the very act of adultery justify herself? Did Jesus give her any psychological excuses? "Woman, how did you get along with your Father when you were a child? Did you receive enough attention and affection?" Jesus didn't justify her on that basis (no one can be justified before God on that basis). If psychology was right, John chapter eight would have been the place for Jesus to demonstrate it. Note the only thing Jesus had to say to her:

Woman, where are your accusers? Hath no man condemned thee? She said, No man, Lord. And Jesus said unto her, Neither do I condemn thee, go and sin no more. (John 8:10-11.)

"Is it man that has condemned thee? Are the bad Pharisees beating you up? Are you in trouble because of racism, bigotry, a disfunctional home, a deprived childhood or early traumas? Is your condemnation because of man?" "No man, Lord." In other words: "I stand here condemned, not by man, not by religion or my race or childhood, or because I am an oppressed woman, or because of a bad relationship with my father, I stand condemned as a sinner before a Holy God, I have broken the Law of God and I admit it!" When she justified God (condemning herself in the process), when she completely acknowledged, "God you are right in your condemnation of me", then (and only then) was Jesus able to completely justify her, *"Neither do I condemn you, go and sin no more."*

This difference between true and false Christians is also illustrated in the story of the two thieves at the crucifixion of Jesus.

But this shall be the covenant that I will make with the house of Israel; after those days, saith the Lord, I will put my law in their inward parts, and write it in their hearts, and will be their God and they shall be my people. (Jeremiah 31:33.)

Real Christianity is far from lawless. Law doesn't save us of course, Christ himself had to die for our sins, once and for all, the just for the unjust, to bring us unto God. But salvation is not lawlessness. It is a new birth in which the law is written not on tables of stone, but in our hearts; those who are truly saved want to obey God. Through the new birth a change takes place in our hearts, our former hostility to the law of God becomes sympathy to it. We want to live lives pleasing to God. This is a miracle, a true sign and wonder! This is not to say that they always end up obeying God, or that salvation means you are no longer selfish at times: Christians can and do fall into sin at times, and the apostle acknowledges such.

My little children, these things I write unto you that you sin not. And if any man sin, we have an advocate with the Father, Jesus Christ the Righteous One, He is the propitiation for our sins, and not for ours only, but also for the sins of the whole world. (I John 2:1-2.)

Sinners must sin, they have no choice, for they are by nature the children of wrath. Christians have the ability to sin, but they have a choice. One of the marks of genuine Christianity is the desire to be obedient to God. Those whose life is marked by the absence of this sign have reason to question their salvation.

THE HATRED OF SIN AS A SIGN

Whosoever committeth sin transgresseth also the law, for sin is the transgression of the law. And ye know that He was manifested to take away our sins, and in Him is no sin. Whosoever abideth in Him sinneth not, whosoever sinneth hath not seen Him, neither known Him, Little children let no man deceive you, he that doeth righteousness is righteous even as He is righteous . . .Whosoever is born of God doth not commit sin, for His seed remaineth in Him: and he cannot sin, because He is born of God. (I John 3:4-9.)

50

As the second sign, the desire to obey the Lord and to keep His commandments is a positive sign of salvation, without which assurance of salvation is dubious. This third sign is the negative aspect of the second. Those who are born again hate sin, therefore they cannot practice it with impunity. As we pointed out in the last section, John is not denying that Christians can and do sin at times. The difference between a Christian and a sinner lies in this: when a Christian sins, part of him hates it. *"His seed remaineth in Him and he cannot sin, because he is born of God."* At the new birth, the very life that condemns sin is imparted unto us – the life of Jesus Christ, who has *"condemned sin in the flesh"*.

The born again Christian is in much the same position as Lazarus was when Jesus spoke unto the grave and called out from among the dead. Lazarus was very much alive, but he was still trapped in His graveclothes. *"Loose him and let him go!"* He had life, and death, he was resurrected but was wrapped up in the bindings of graveclothes; life on the inside and death on the outside. Just like you and I, being born again doesn't eradicate the wrong and even sinful thought patterns, the unrenewed mindset, our external graveclothes. But we do receive life on a deeper level, and that life cannot abide sin.

When John tells us that *"whosoever abideth in Him sinneth not,"* or that *"whosoever is born of God doth not commit sin",* He is not contradicting his earlier statement that *"If any man sin we have an advocate with the Father".* God knows that Christians can and do sin and He has graciously made provision for this. What *is* He saying then? He is saying that the truly born again cannot habitually practice sin, they cannot sin consistently with impunity, they have an abiding seed in them that hates sin and wants out of it. Whoever is a stranger to this hatred of sin has no reason to believe that they have ever known God.

LOVE IS ESSENTIAL TO CHRISTIANITY

We know that we have passed from death unto life, because we love the brethren. He that loveth not His brother abideth in death, Whosoever hateth his brother is a murderer, and ye know that no murderer hath eternal life abiding in Him. (I John 3:14.)

God is Love, therefore Christianity is Love. Those who have been touched by God have been touched by love. Christians love. I know people who say "I love God but I hate the church." Such people have no reason to believe that they are saved.

If a man say, I Love God and hates his brother is a liar. For he that loveth not His brother whom he hath seen, how can he love God whom he hath not seen? And this commandment have we from him, that He who loves God love his brother also. (I John 4:20-21.)

Love and forgiveness are so essential, that those who won't practice them have no valid assurance of salvation.

TRUE CHRISTIANS OVERCOME THE WORLD

For whatsoever is born of God overcomes the world: and this is the victory that overcomes the world, even our faith. Who is he that overcometh the world, but he that believeth that Jesus is the Son of God. (I John 5:4-5.)

When I was a new Christian, I had a very basic understanding of what "worldliness" meant. It was quite simple, there were worldly styles of clothing, worldly music, worldly habits (drinking, smoking, dancing, fornicating, etc.). In short, to my understanding, worldliness was a very external concept. To be worldly was to look, think, or act in a certain fashion. This is a superficial way to understand the biblical concept of worldliness.

52

Love not the world, neither the things that are in the world, if any man love the world, the love of the Father is not in him, for all that is in the world, the lust of the flesh, and the lust of the eyes, and the pride of life, is not of the Father, but is of the world. And the world passeth away, and the lust thereof, but he that doeth the will of God abideth forever. (I John 2:15-17.)

As we know and believe in the Holy Trinity – Father, Son and Holy Spirit, so there is an unholy Trinity, which is the world, the flesh, and the devil. The Unholy Trinity has ranged itself in opposition to the Holy Trinity, as the Scriptures teach. For example, we know that *"The flesh lusteth against the spirit".* And we know that Satan himself directly opposed the Lord Jesus Christ, in the days of His flesh, and will seek to do so again in the time of the Anti-christ. And in the above passage we can see that those who receive the love of the world, cannot have the love of the Father. The world is a spiritual reality, which manifests itself in outward things, some of those things being obviously evil, and others, being "good". The evils of the world are obvious to most Christians, the danger to us is that we not be snared by the "good" of this world! In the end, the struggle will not be blatant evil versus Glorious good, it will be far more subtle, Good versus "good". The Good, as personified in Jesus Christ, who said, *"Why do you call me good, there is none good but God." (Luke 19),* as opposed to the "good" of a world which seeks to exist independently of God; for that is the meaning of the term 'the world'. "The world" which we are to *"love not . . . neither the things of . . ."* is none other than the order of human life, with all of its values, aspirations and beliefs, which seeks to exist independently of the holy, personal God of the Bible. The things of the world which John describes are spiritual also. The three characteristics seem to hearken back to the description of that critical moment in the garden of Eden when the fate of Adam and Eve (and the whole of humanity) hung in the balance, when a decision was being made.

And when the woman saw that the tree was good for food . . . . . . (Lust of the flesh)
And that it was pleasant to the eyes . . . . (Lust of the eyes)
and a tree to be desired to make one wise . . . . (Boastful pride of Life)
she took of the fruit thereof, and did eat, and gave also unto her husband with her and He did eat. (Genesis 3: 6.)

This is the essence of worldliness, not in what she actually did, but in the decision made, to act for herself, independently and defiantly of God. God had decreed to her and her husband, that in the day they would eat of the tree they would surely die. They had the Word of God. But Genesis 3:6 tells us that Eve made her own judgments on the situation. "I know what the Bible says about that fruit, *but it looks good to me.*" This was the birth of the world system, not in something as outwardly drastic as murder or fornication, but as simple as making an independent judgment, in defiance of the revealed will of God.

Worldliness is about a perspective of life that excludes God. Therefore there can be a worldly goodness, a humanism, even a worldly form of Christianity! Cain showed this when he sought to worship God on His own terms, once again in defiance of the Word, the revealed Word of God. The contrast between the world and the Kingdom, is stark – as laid out opposite.

WORLDLY VALUES	KINGDOM VALUES
The temporal, live for today.	The eternal.
Sovereignty of man *(Psalm 2:1-3.)*	Sovereignty of God.
Man the measure of all things.	All things made for God's pleasure.
Basic problems in world: ignorance, poverty, inequality.	Basic problems: Man has rebelled against a holy, personal God.
The ends justify the means. Make your own judgment.	It is written . . .
People are basically good.	There is none good but God.
Man is evolving into a higher state, he can save himself!	Man has fallen, but can be redeemed.
"I will . . . I will . . . I will . . ."	Not my will, but thine be done.
We can get back to Eden (Utopia).	I want to go to heaven.
Self is central . . . State is central.	God is supreme.

A simple summation of the difference between worldly values and Kingdom values is found in the description in the New Testament, of what is called the two mysteries, *The Mystery of Godliness* and *The Mystery of Iniquity*. For these are the two contrasting value systems, the only two religions, they are the final dividing line that shall separate everyone in the world.

And without controversy, great is the Mystery of Godliness, God was manifested in the flesh . . . (I Timothy 3:16.)

For the mystery of iniquity doth already work . . . who opposeth and exalteth himself above all that is called God, or that is worshipped; so that He as God sitteth in the temple of God, shewing himself that He is God . . . (II Thessalonians 2:7, 4.)

The mystery, or spiritual principle of iniquity, is the idea that a man can ascend to the level of God. This is the dynamic underlying Hinduism, Buddhism, animism and atheism, not to mention humanism, and every other false religion. Supposedly, we can rise up, we can be gods! Yoga, masonry, the mystery religions, reincarnation, evolution, science of mind and countless others all in one way or another testify that man is ascending, he is rising unto higher levels, constantly evolving. This "mystery" has animated the universal rebellion against the God of the Bible. From the time Lucifer proclaimed his infamous "I wills" (Isaiah 14), to Adam and Eve's trampling of faithfulness and grateful love to God in the dirt in their quest to be "as god", down to the Tower of Babel, right up to our present "New Age movement" and "New World order", man's imagination has clung to the vain idea that we can do it ourselves, that we don't need God; we don't have to be under Him; we can make our own judgments, set our own limits, and even create our own millennium! This is called in the Bible, *the Delusion*, *the Lie* that mankind has been susceptible to, which will ultimately result in the "strong delusion" by which God will ultimately judge the unbelieving world.

Even Him whose coming is after the working of Satan with all power and signs and lying wonders, and with all deceivableness of unrighteousness in them that perish: because they receive not the **love of the truth***, that they might be saved. And for this cause God shall send them strong delusion, that they should* **believe a Lie and be damned** *. . ."* *(II Thessalonians 2:9-12.)*

And what is this faith that allows us to overcome the world, this mystery of godliness? If the lie is that man can be a god, the truth that saves us and changes our values, nature, worldview and every part of our inner life, is the opposite. Man cannot be other than man. Made in the Image of God, yes, but a created being, a worshipper of the one true God, a finite creation under God. But God became a man, *God was manifested in the flesh.* God became a man, when Jesus Christ came in the flesh.

The most worldly thing anyone ever did in the Bible was when Adam and Eve ate of the forbidden fruit, because they were in effect saying "Not Thy will, but mine be done!" The most unworldly thing anyone ever did in the Bible was when Jesus Christ struggled in another garden, the garden of Gethsemane, not wanting to go to the cross, but more than that, wanting to obey the Father and save our souls. *"Not my will, but thine be done!"* In the one case, created beings strove to ascend up unto God's level, to be "In God's class of being", as Kenneth Hagin and the faith-teachers assert. In the other case, the infinite, personal, Holy God of the Bible humbled Himself to be a man, and to die our deaths as a sinner! It is this faith that changes us and allows us to overcome the world!

And no man has ascended unto heaven, but he that came down from heaven, even the Son of man which is in heaven. (John 3:13.)

False religion has man rising up, climbing the ladder to heaven, ascending the holy mountain, striving to attain a position. The faith that overcomes this world is based on the truth that we are so bankrupt, so lost in sin, that we could never rise up, we could never attain to the level of God. If we are to be saved, God must come down unto us, He must condescend to our level, *"Jesus Christ has come* [and remains] *in the flesh."*

THE FIVE SIGNS IN REVIEW

By these signs of the saving work of God's spirit, we can "Test ourselves to see if we be in the faith". They have to do with changes in our heart. These are not works that anybody can do, they are dispositions of the heart, born of the Holy Spirit. Once again they are:

1. True Christians justify God	I John 1:5-10
2. True Christians want to obey God	I John 2
3. True Christians hate sin, and cannot practice sin with impunity	I John 3
4. True Christians love the brethren	I John 3:14
5. True Christians overcome the world	I John 5.

CHAPTER 5

CONCERNING THE ANTICHRIST

And every spirit that confesseth not that Jesus Christ is come in the flesh is not of God; and this is the spirit of anti-christ, whereof you have heard that it should come; and even now already is it in the world. (I John 4:2.)

Who is a liar but He that denieth that Jesus is the Christ? He is anti-christ, that denieth the Father and the Son. Whoever denieth the Son the same hath not the Father. (I John 2:22-23.)

John presents the Anti-christ in two ways, First, as a spiritual principle, a *spirit of anti-christ*, which has been working in the world at least since the days of the apostles, if not earlier. Secondly he presents the Anti-christ as a person, a denier of the Father and the Son. There is a spirit of anti-christ which has been in the world, working for a long time against the purposes of God, but it will be culminated in a particular person, the Anti-Christ, who must be revealed in the last time.

Popular culture has developed a literature concerning the Anti-christ, which fosters a deception and a horror movie Anti-christ, who is terrifying to behold, bloody, perhaps with fangs, arched eyebrows and a goatee beard — an obviously evil archetype, openly demonic, trying to induce people to "take the mark". On the contrary, the Anti-christ will be "good". He will personify the epitome of human aspirations of goodness. Far from being demonic, he will present himself as

"Christian". His coming will not be overtly satanic, it will seem for a brief time as though finally the religious longings of the human race, "peace on earth and good will toward men", perhaps might be realised through the efforts of this man! To question this humble servant will seem to be the height of arrogance and bigotry. When you think Antichrist, quit thinking Adolph Hitler, Stalin or perhaps Bela Lagosi; start thinking Norman Vincent Peale, Robert Schuller or perhaps Mother Teresa! The final Battle will not be the obvious "Good against Evil", rather it will be a subtle "good against good".

Part of the problem comes from a misunderstanding of the very name, "Anti-christ". Too many of us take the prefix "anti-" to mean "against", as if he is the "against Christ". But the prefix "anti-" doesn't always mean "against", it can also mean "instead of". The Anti-christ doesn't represent a total all out assault against Christ, rather he is a subtle "substitute Christ", a replacement Christ. Jesus warned us in John 5,

I am come in my Father's name, and ye receive me not, if another shall come in his own name, him you shall receive. (John 5: 43.)

The Christ of God, is the one who truly came "in the Father's name", which means He came on the basis of the terms that the Father had set forth, ie, he fulfilled prophecies, he spoke the Word of God, he did the things that the Father had said that the Christ would do. In spite of the fact that He truly did come in the Father's name, he was (and is) rejected by those who should have known better, the people of God. They didn't like to imagine a Christ who would call for their repentance, or who would come and suffer and be rejected, they wanted a worldly Christ, a political, triumphalistic Christ who would overthrow the Romans. The freedom they desired was not the freedom from the dominion of sin that Christ offered, they had other ideals!

They were "already free" remember? The consequence of rejecting Christ is that you end up accepting in one form or another "Anti-christ". *"Another will come in his own name, him you will receive."*

TYPES OF ANTI-CHRIST

John warned us that even in His time, there were *many anti-christs,* and yet all of them pointed to the ultimate Anti-christ. In Scripture, Christ has been foreshadowed by certain Old Testament figures and events. Abel, Isaac, Joseph, King David, and all of the prophets in some way or another were types of Christ. In the same way there have been many figures who have foreshadowed the Anti-christ, as a warning and a teaching of what He would be like, that He might be recognised and avoided.

Cain is the first example of the "man of lawlessness", the anti-Abel, who substituted the produce of the ground, for the bloody sacrifice that Abel offered unto God. In this way he teaches us that the Anti-christ will not represent secularism, but he will be religious, a worshipper of God as creator, but will ignore the need for redemption by the Blood. We are warned in Jude,

Woe unto them, for they have gone in the way of Cain! (Jude 11.)

As Cain persecuted Abel for being accepted by God through blood, so the Anti-christ will make war with the saints and even prevail over them, for a time.

Lamech also, the sixth generation from Cain, who boasted in Genesis 4 that he would avenge himself far greater and for far less of an offence than the vengeance God promised to protect Cain with, also teaches us something of the Anti-christ. As Cain was the substitute Abel, Lamech is the "anti-Enoch", the boastful opposite of everything godly Enoch stood for.

And Lamech said unto His wives, Adah and Zillah, Hear my voice; ye wives of Lamech, hearken unto my speech: for I have slain a man to my wounding, and a young man to my hurt, If Cain shall be avenged sevenfold, truly Lamech seventy and seven fold. (Genesis 4:23-24.)

Proud boasting, particularly against the God of Heaven, is one of the marks of the Anti-christ, as Daniel, Revelation and II Thessalonians testify to.

And he shall speak great words against the Most High. (Daniel 7:25.)

Who opposes and exalts himself above all that is called God, or that is worshipped; so that He as God sitteth in the temple of God, showing himself that He is God. (II Thessalonians 2:4)

And he opened His mouth in Blasphemy against God, to blaspheme His name, and His tabernacle, and them that dwell in Heaven. (Revelation 13:6.)

Nimrod also teaches us something about the Anti-christ, because his very name means "Let us Rebel". The Anti-christ, like Nimrod, will unite the whole world (isn't that the universal longing being expressed these days?). He will seek to undo the so called "Babel effect", the division of the Nations instituted by God. This is the political expression of the Anti-christ spirit!

There are many others. Balaam, who learned that the people of God cannot be destroyed overtly by curses or any kind of occult power, but must be seduced into corrupting themselves through fornication and compromise with idolatry. In some way the Anti-christ will draw the church into an ecumenical and interfaith unity which will amount to spiritual adultery and fornication. There are many Balaams within the church working to make this a current reality.

Pharaoh, Nebuchadnezzar, the Caesars and any other world rulers who received worship as gods, are types of the coming Anti-christ, as are the Popes, who actually take the title "Christus Vicarus", the vicars (substitutes) of Christ. The *vicarus* prefix in Latin has the same meaning as the *anti* prefix in Greek, they both mean "substitute fo".. All of these point to their ultimate fulfilment, the one who is coming, who will embody the universal rebellion against God, and His Christ which Psalm 2 foretells,

Why do the heathen rage, and the people imagine a vain thing? The kings of the earth set themselves, and the rulers take council together against the Lord and His Christ, saying, 'Let us break their bands asunder, and cast away their cords from us'.

OTHER NAMES AND TITLES

He is only called "Anti-christ" by John. But there are other names and titles for Him. He is called "the man of Lawlessness", because He personifies the world wide rebellion against God, He is called the "Son of Perdition", because He is sure to go to Hell, also "the lawless One", "the Opposer", "the Beast", "The little Horn". These are seven names for Him, although there may be even more. The types are numerous. The one type of Anti-christ which John was actually closest to, and perhaps had in mind when he warned us of him, was Judas. Judas teaches us of what the Anti-christ will be like. He also was called "The Son of Perdition".

JUDAS, WHO WENT OUT FROM US

How is Judas like the Anti-christ? First of all Judas was a Christian. The Anti-christ will come out of some kind of Christianity, or perhaps better put, Christendom. Judas was a messianic believer in Jesus, who lived with Him, heard his teaching, preached in His name and cast out devils and healed in His name! The Anti-christ also will come in a "signs and wonders" mode that will appear to many to be "Christian".

Even Him, whose coming is after the working of Satan with all power and signs and lying wonders . . . (II Thessalonians 2:10.)

Perhaps John was remembering the events He witnessed on the night of the last supper, when Jesus announced the presence of the betrayer. None of those who were there knew who the betrayer was, in fact the faithful disciples questioned themselves, "Is it I?" Jesus did reveal the identity of the betrayer to two of the disciples, but the rest were clueless. Even so, in these last days, discernment is at an all-time low, the spirit of anti-christ is supping at the very table with us, and a good many in the company of the faithful, are oblivious to it. They know there is a betrayer, but have no idea that they may well be sitting right next to him.

When Judas actually did go out into the night, most of the disciples thought He had gone out to give charity to the poor, this because Judas had given them this impression on other occasions.

Then saith one of His disciples, Judas Iscariot, Simon's son, which should betray Him, Why was not this ointment sold for three hundred pence and given to the poor? (John 12:3.)

The Anti-christ will not appear to be a Hitler or a Stalin, he will pass himself off as a philanthropist, a do-gooder, a religious person, someone who cares about the poor and needy. He will also make sure everyone knows that He loves Jesus. Remember how Judas betrayed Him? With a Kiss.

Little Children, it is the last time, and as ye have heard that anti-christ shall come even now are there many anti-christs; whereby we know that it is the last time. They went out from us, but they were not of us. (I John 2:18-19.)

The final betrayal of Christ will come not from atheists, New Agers, Buddhists or Hindus, for they cannot betray Christ, they have never professed any allegiance to Him. The Anti-christ, like Judas, will be someone who appears to be Christian, a powerful "cutting edged" Christian at that, replete with "signs and wonder", he's got the stuff! He will appear also to be benevolent, compassionate, a real do-gooder. Most Christians will have no idea who he is, but the faithful will know. He will give "lip service" to Jesus, as long as he needs to, but he will distort the doctrine of Christ, he will seek in some way to spiritualise Christ, to deny some aspect of the Incarnation. A dis-incarnate Christ, a spiritualised anointing, attended with signs and wonders such as the world has never seen them, will be part of how he seduces the elect (as many as possible) into the new religion. The current signs and wonders movement, with its dis-incarnate "glory", that people are willing to make pilgrimages to partake of, seems to be a good candidate for the "delusion" spoken of in conjunction with Paul's Words about the Anti-christ is II Thessalonians 2.

Mending the Nets

Part II

Verse by verse

through

I JOHN

I John

CHAPTER 1

That which was from the beginning, which we have heard, which we have seen with our eyes, which we have looked upon and our hands have handled, of the Word of Life; (for the Life was manifested, and we have seen it, and bear witness, and shew unto you that eternal life, which was with the Father, and was manifested unto us;) (I John 1:1-2.)

As in his gospel, John opens up his discussion at the beginning, for the one whom they had actually handled, touched, seen with their eyes, Jesus of Nazareth, is indeed God come to us in the flesh. Only of God could it be said that He was *from the beginning.* John strongly refutes Docetism here by emphasising the physical Incarnation of the Word of Life. This *Logos* of life came from the Father in eternity, and dwelt among us in history in such a way that the apostles touched him physically!

That which we have seen and heard declare we unto you, that you also may have fellowship with us: and truly our fellowship is with the Father and with His Son, Jesus Christ. And these things write we unto you, that your joy may be full. (I John 1:3-4.)

By his writing and preaching, the goal John has is twofold. Ever the evangelist, John would bring us into the fellowship He himself had been introduced into, fellowship with the Father and His Son Jesus! This was the primary aim of John's gospel. But John is also a pastor and through this epistle he seeks to perfect the joy of those of us who have already entered the fellowship. This joy, springing out of our fellowship with the Father and His Son, is in danger of being stunted and even robbed through artificial spirituality, pseudo-christianity supplanting the true life.

This then is the message which we have heard of Him and declare unto you, that God is light and in Him is no darkness at all. (I John 1:5.)

John isn't innovating here, this is the true summary of the message that the Word of Life, who came into history in the person of Jesus Christ, delivered to the apostles. It is a revelation concerning the nature of the true God. *God is light and in Him is no darkness at all.* God is not said to be the light, God *is* light! John Stott's comments are helpful here:

Of the statements about the essential being of God, none is more comprehensive than *God is light.* It is His nature to reveal Himself, as it is the property of light to shine; and the revelation is of perfect purity and unutterable majesty. We are to think of God as a personal being, infinite in all of His perfections, transcendent . . . yet who desires to be known and has revealed Himself

(J.R.W. Stott *Letters of John,* Tyndale NT Commentaries, Eerdmans.)

If we say that we have fellowship with Him and walk in darkness we lie and do not the truth: But if we walk in the light, as he is in the light, we have fellowship with one another and the blood of Jesus Christ his Son cleanses us from all sin." (I John 1:6-7.)

This is the first of three "If we say"s that John cites to refute the false claims of the heretics. To walk in the light is to walk "out in the open", fully revealed, no secrets, willing to be known just as you are. This is Christianity, for *God is light.* To walk in darkness is to have a secret, unrevealed life, a life marked by denial, particularly the denial of sin or the sin nature. To walk in the light does not imply a walk of sinless perfection, otherwise why would the benefit of walking in the light be the ongoing continuous cleansing of each and every sin? This is the Greek sense of verse 7. Being sincere, open, transparent and realistic about sin, enables us to remain in fellowship with Jesus and consequently with one another.

If we say that we have no sin, we deceive ourselves, and the truth is not in us. If we confess our sins, he is faithful and just to forgive us our sins, and to cleanse us from all unrighteousness. (I John 1:8-9.)

Here John refutes the error that we have no sin nature, by using the word sin in the singular. To the Gnostic perversion of Christianity, the removal of sin is not the main issue, but rather the removal of ignorance. Reconciliation with a holy, personal God, through the sacrifice of His Son on the cross, is not the focal point, instead the emphasis is on discovery of the spiritual self, through the gnosis, the "revelation knowledge". In one way or another the Gnostics deny the sin nature. "Drop that old 'sinner' label, you are the righteousness of God in Christ!" say the faith-teachers, misquoting 2 Corinthians 5:21. One musician, influenced by the faith-teachers, couldn't even bring himself to sing the first stanza of *Amazing Grace* correctly, because of the line "That saved *a wretch* like me", he changed it to "That saved *someone* like me".

The confession of sins, *homologeia* – "to say the same things as" God – about our sins is the only prerequisite for complete forgiveness and cleansing. Note that such forgiveness and cleansing are a matter of His faithfulness and justice, not of our feelings. When all rationalisations, renaming of sins, and excuses for them are dropped and we get down to the level of frank acknowledgment, "I have sinned, I have lied, I have stolen, Lord, I have lusted and even coveted . . .", in short, when we say the same things about our sins as He says of them, we are forgiven and cleansed by our faithful and righteous High Priest!

If we say that we have not sinned, we make Him a liar, and His Word is not in us. (I John 1:10.)

We must all justify and condemn at the same time, the only question is, who will we end up justifying and who will we condemn? Those who justify themselves, do so at the expense of condemning God. In order to justify God (admit that He is, and has been right in His evaluation of our lives) we must, of necessity, condemn ourselves. If God is right, we have been wrong, if instead it is you who have been in the right, God is wrong because he declares that we have *"all sinned and are coming short of the Glory of God."* (Romans 3:23.) *"Let God be true and every man a liar, that you might be justified when you speak, and overcome when you are judged."* (Romans 3:4.)

I JOHN

CHAPTER 2

My little children I write these things unto you that you sin not. And if any man sin, we have an advocate with the Father, Jesus Christ the righteous and He is the propitiation for our sins, and not for our sins only, but also for the sins of the whole world. (I John 2:1-2.)

I John 2:1-2 gives us a perfect balance, concerning the sin issue. *"I write these things unto you that you sin not."* This reflects the revelation that, *"God is light".* Don't sin by denying the existence of a sin nature or that individual sins keep us from fellowship with God; don't condemn God by contradicting His universal indictment that *"there is none good . . . all have sinned and come short . . ."* And in the light of the ready forgiveness offered to those who confess, don't accept a casual attitude towards sin and forgiveness. *"I write these things unto you that you sin not."*

But *"God is love"* also, therefore *"If any man does sin."* God knows what we are and He has acknowledged our weakness and vulnerability. *"We have an advocate with the Father",* note that the apostle includes himself in this, God has made provision for His little children who, though they hate sin, and are born again, are at times subject to temptations of the flesh and of this world, and even attacks from the wicked one. He has appointed an Advocate, a *paraclete,* one called alongside to help at the judgment seat, none other than *"Jesus Christ the righteous One, the propitiation for our sins . . ."* If we do sin we have a great high priest, *"in the flesh"*, that is, fully conversant with the range of human experience, temptation, discouragement, suffering, sorrow, and weariness.

He pleads for us at the throne of God as the *"propitiation for our sins".* This word *propitiation* presupposes two elements, our guilt and God's wrath. God loves us as His dear children, but He has never stopped hating sin in all of its forms. We have an advocate, a mediator, who has made himself our propitiation offering to God! This means an appeasement, a satisfaction offering. His sinless life, perfectly pleasing to the Father, offered for ours, is the only offering that could possibly satisfy the requirements of a holy and righteous God, in the light of our transgression. His was the only life of whom God could declare, *"This is my beloved Son in whom I am well pleased."* In the prime of His life, *"He who knew no sin, was made to be sin for us, that we might be the righteousness of God in Christ."* Now Jesus is our ever-righteous priest seated at the right hand of God, in perpetual right-standing with God. As Peter said, He died to *"bring us to God",* once and for all, in one sense, but in another sense, He brings us to God in an ongoing relationship; *"He ever lives to make intercession for us."* You and I can never satisfy the demands of the holiness of God, nor the righteous requirements of His will, not even at our best! But this One who is our advocate has offered an offering which actually has satisfied the righteous demands of our Holy Father and which is eternally effectual. God can look at what Jesus offered for us and be satisfied forever.

And hereby we do know that we know Him, if we keep His commandments. He that saith, I know Him and keepeth not His commandments is a liar and the truth is not in Him. But whoso keepeth His word, in Him verily is the love of God perfected: hereby know we that we are in Him. (I John 2:3-5.)

Do you want to have assurance of salvation? Whoever is really saved has a desire to keep God's commandments. Whoever cares not to obey the revealed will of God, and yet claims to know God, is a liar, and devoid of the truth. Note that John connects being perfected in love, with keeping God's commandments. This addresses the artificial division between love and God's laws. Gnostic thought, (and a good deal of modern thought as well) set forth a sharp dualism between love and law, as though they are opposites. "We aren't into law brother, we are into love!" But to John, and the other apostles, love and law go together. To keep His commandments is to keep His Word, and whoever keeps His Word, in Him verily is the love of God perfected! Love is not antinomian *(lawless)*. And concern for obeying God's Word is not to be confused with *legalism*. John is not saying that we are saved by lawkeeping, he has already pointed to the great *"propitiation for our sins"*. Law is not a means of salvation to us, but because we are saved, and the law has been written in our hearts by the Holy Ghost, we now want to obey the teaching of our Redeemer out of gratitude. The Law of God is now the teaching of how to love, the measure of whether or not, and to what extent, I love God or neighbour. *"If you love me, keep my commandments."*

He that saith He abideth in Him ought himself also so to walk, even as He walked. (I John 2:6.)

We never read where Jesus called all of the disciples together to hug them or to tell them how much he loved them. But mention Jesus and people automatically think love. The command to walk even as Jesus walked, means nothing less than to walk in love.

Brethren, I write no new commandment unto you, but an old commandment which ye had from the beginning. The old commandment is the Word which ye have heard from the beginning. Again, a new commandment I write unto you, which thing is true in

74

Him and in you: because the darkness is past and the true light now shineth. (I John 2:7-8.)

The commandment to love is not new in one sense, it is *"from the beginning".* In another sense it is new, because with the coming of Jesus, *"the true light now shines".* The appeal of Gnosticism, and all other false spiritualities, is the appeal of the new. We don't bring a new doctrine or experience, we call for love, love for God and man, according to God's word. The Law of Moses told us that we are to *"Love the Lord our God with all of our hearts, with all of our souls, and with all of our minds",* and in another place we are exhorted to *"love your neighbour as yourself".*

On the other hand this commandment is new, because with the coming of Jesus, *the true light,* we have a practical example, even a personal experience of this love. He is the very embodiment of the commandment to Love God supremely and all others equally. The one who has *"loved us and washed us from our sins in His own blood",* calls us to follow in His steps, to also love God supremely, and to love our neighbour, only this time, not merely as we love ourselves, but *"as I [Jesus] have loved you.* This love, which He has shown unto us, when we were His enemy, we are to let transform us.

He that saith he is in the light and hateth His brother is in darkness even until now. He that loveth his brother abideth in the light and there is no occasion of stumbling in Him. But he that hateth his brother is in darkness and walketh in darkness and knoweth not whether he goeth, because that darkness has blinded his eyes. (I John 2:9-11.)

Hatred of anyone, particularly of a brother, is incompatible with Christianity. Christians may be offended at times, they may lose control of their tongues, they may say or do things they regret later, but anyone who can abide in hatred has no reason to believe they are *in the light.*

Note that John mentions *abiding* in the light. It is possible to be in the light, but to become offended, to the point where you leave the light to *walk in darkness*. There are those who are not Christian at all, but imagine themselves to be so, although their blatant hatred of others belies them. Then there are those who at one time were *in the light*, like Judas, but who allowed bitterness to become hatred and who consequently went out into the darkness. This verse is a warning as well as a test. Love allows us to see; hatred blinds us, it robs us of judgment, it distorts our viewpoint.

I write unto you little children, because your sins are forgiven you for His name's sake. I write unto you fathers because you have known Him that is from the beginning. I write unto you young men because you have overcome the wicked One. I write unto you little children, because you have known the Father. I have written unto you fathers because you have known Him that is from the beginning. I have written unto you young men, because you are strong and the Word of God abides in you, and ye have overcome the wicked One. (I John 2:12-14.)

This letter wasn't written to heretics though, it was written to the church, and to all levels of believers, of which John gives three classifications, *children, fathers,* and *young men.* He would confirm our faith and sharpen our discernment, he hasn't written to tear us down, he has written to assure our hearts before God. There are two different words for children, *teknia,* which he uses in the first instance, and *paidia* in the second. To the *teknia,* the newborn, forgiveness of our sins is assured, the tense is perfect, "You have been and remain forgiven." To the *paidia,* those under discipline, "You have come to know the Father,"

To the fathers in the church, those who have matured in Christ and begotten others through the Gospel, who are adult in their Christian life, twice he assures, *"you have known Him that is from the beginning".* The everlasting, unchanging, eternal God is who you have come to know.

They have deepened in their faith and in the knowledge of God, His person, attributes, faithfulness, and truth.

To the young men, spiritually speaking, those who have been in Christ long enough to become settled in the reality of the forgiveness of sins and their adoption as sons by the Father, who therefore have entered into the spiritual warfare of Christian life, John assures, *"you are strong and have overcome the wicked One"*. What is the source of this strength to win battles over Satan, the world and the flesh? *"The Word of God abides in you."*

Love not the World, neither the things that are in the world, if any man loves the world, the love of the Father is not in Him. For all that is in the world, the lust of the flesh, and the lust of the eyes, and the pride of life, is not of the Father, but is of the world. And the world passeth away, and the lust thereof, but he that doeth the will of God abideth forever. (I John 2:15-17.)

In contrast to the children, young men, and fathers of the church John has just addressed, whose values have been shaped by the fact that they *"know the Father"*, and *"He who is from the beginning"*, who by submitting to the Word of God have overcome the wicked One, and whose sins are forgiven, John would turn our attention to the world.

"Love not the world." What is it that the apostles and our Lord refer to in their warning to us about the dangers inherent in the world? "The world" refers to none other than all of society and human life which is established on the basis of independence of the God of the Bible. It includes the institutions, values, ideals, hopes, aspirations, thoughts, dreams and religions of all of life lived away from God. It does not limit itself to externals, such as music styles, clothing, dances, alcohol and tobacco. The world is a spiritual state, a mindset. It has its obvious

bad, but it also includes good. In fact it is the good aspect of the world that is most dangerous and deceptive. The essence of the term world is that it is a system, a culture of independence from God.

As there is a Holy Trinity, of Father, Son and Holy Spirit, there is an unholy Trinity of the world, the flesh, and the devil. We know from Galatians, that *"the flesh lusteth against the Spirit"*. Satan personally opposes Jesus Christ, and sought to turn Him away from the cross on many occasions. Now we learn that one of the reasons we are to *"love not the world"*, is because the love for and of the world and the Love of the Father are mutually exclusive. One cannot have both the love of the lorld and the love of the Father. We are told in the rest of the bible that the World is hostile to Christ, cannot receive the Holy Spirit, will believe anything but the Truth, and will also be hostile to and reject the children of God. James tells us that to be a friend of the world is to be an enemy of the Father!

Another reason we are to *"love not the World"*, is because it is temporary. This world, contrary to the popular message we hear over and over again these days, is not going to be made into a better place, it is a world under judgment; it is doomed as the world was in the days of Noah, and there is no going back. In fact the death of Jesus on the cross constituted *"the judgment of this world"*.

Now is the judgment of this world, now shall the prince of this world be cast out. And I, if I be lifted up from the earth, will draw all men unto me. (John 12:31-32.)

Little children, it is the last time: and as ye have heard that anti-christ shall come, even now are there many anti-christs; whereby we know that it is the last time. (I John 2:18.)

ERRATA: page 49 - after paragraph 4 ...of Jesus) insert:

And one of the malefactors which were hanged railed on him saying, If Thou be the Christ save thyself and us. But the other answering rebuked Him saying, Dost not Thou fear God, seeing Thou art in the same condemnation? And we indeed justly; for we recieve the due reward of our deeds; but this man has done nothing amiss. And he said, Lord Jesus, remember me when you come into your Kingdom. And Jesus said unto Him, verily I say unto thee, today thou shalt be with me in Paradise. (Luke 23:39-43.)

Note the contrast between the two thieves' approaches to God. To the first thief, God is supposed to be there to get you out of trouble, "If you are Christ, save yourself and us." No mention of sin, righteousness or judgment, no acknowledgment of the broken law of God, simply "Get us out of here!". But the second thief justified God, confessing that both he and the first thief deserved their own condemnation, but that Jesus had done nothing wrong. This is the mark of a true Christian, because it takes the Holy Spirit to get anyone to that point.

TRUE CHRISTIANS WANT TO OBEY GOD

And hereby we know that we know Him if we keep His commandments. He that saith, I know Him, and keepeth not His commandments, is a liar and the truth is not in Him. (1 John 2:3-4.)

One of the greatest signs of the New Birth is the desire to obey God. The Prophets spoke of this desire to obey as being part of the New Covenant that God would give to Israel. As opposed to the Law being written on tables of stone, God has promised that He would 'write the law on our hearts', and birth in us a desire to walk in His ways.

A new heart also will I give you and a new spirit will I put within you: and I will take away the stony heart out of your flesh, and I will give you a heart of flesh. And I will put my spirit within you and cause you to walk in my statutes and you shall keep my judgments and do them. (Ezekiel 36:26-27.)

Closely associated with the concept of the world, and in relation to the last days, John warns of both the Anti-christ to come and of the many anti-christs. The prefix "anti" can mean both "against", and also "instead of". The word "Christ" is the Greek word for the Hebrew "Messiah", which means "anointed One". An anti-christ is a "substitute Christ", a falsely anointed one. There have always been many who have boasted of a false anointing, but as the last days approach, they multiply. All anti-christs point to the ultimate Anti-christ, described in Daniel and Revelation, the one Paul spoke of as *"the man of sin, the Son of perdition"*. *(2 Thessalonians 2:1-9.)*

They went out from us, but they were not of us; for if they had been of us, they would no doubt have continued with us: but they went out, that they might be manifest that they were not all of us. (I John 2:19.)

John uses the same word here for *went out* (Greek: *exelthan*) as he did in John 13 to describe Judas going out into the night to betray Jesus. Like Judas, the falsely anointed ones came out from the midst of us (the church). They are particularly dangerous because they know our language, they ate and drank with us, they have an understanding of our thinking, but the fact that they don't remain in fellowship with us manifests that they are not of us! They sell the Truth for thirty pieces of silver. They had to leave the church, they couldn't stay; all has to be manifested (see Proverbs 18:1). Those who are really of us may fall, but by grace they shall persevere.

But you have an unction from the Holy One and ye know all things. I have not written unto you because you know not the truth, but because you know it and that no lie is of the truth. (I John 2:20-21.)

In contrast to the falsely anointed, whose proud boasts of great spiritual prowess had tempted the elect to doubt their own experience, the apostle assures us that it is we who truly have an unction, an anointing of the Spirit which we have all received upon conversion. This *charisma* is an unction to know things. We needn't be enamoured of the pseudo-christs, who offer new anointings and secret knowledge. We have an unction from God himself, and it is an anointing that we might know all we need to know. And we do know the truth, there are no "hidden secrets to successful spiritual empowerment". He who knows and believes in the simple Gospel needs no guru, through the Spirit we know everything we need to know already. And furthermore what we know, the gospel, is completely sincere, *"for no lie is of the truth"*. There isn't one truth for a lower level of Christian, another "deeper" truth for those who are more advanced.

Who is a liar but he that denieth that Jesus is the Christ? He is antichrist, that denieth the Father and the Son. (I John 2:22.)

This verse is literally translated *"who is the liar?"* The arch lie is some form of a denial of the doctrine of Christ. There are many variations of this denial, but all variations mark the bearer of this distortion out as antichrist. Many commentators believe that John was speaking of the adoptionist heresy, which is the false teaching that Jesus was a man who for a brief time (three and one half years), was "enchristed". In other words he wasn't *the* Christ; the Spirit came upon him at his baptism, but lifted from him before he went to the cross. The conclusion being, anyone could have the same anointing and do the same things Jesus did. Another candidate for this was Docetism: Jesus really wasn't a man, he only seemed to be one, (*docein* - to seem). Therefore he felt no pain, never tired, really didn't die on the cross. He never came to us *"in the flesh"*. As John Stott says in his excellent Tyndale commentary:

The heretic's theology is not just defective, it is diabolical. The fundamental doctrinal test of a professing Christian concerns his views of the person of Jesus.

(Stott, *Letters of John*, Tyndale NT Commentaries, Eerdmans p.116.)

Whosoever denieth the Son, the same hath not the Father: but he that acknowledges the Son hath the Father also. (I John 2:23.)

Who says doctrine is unimportant? It is so significant to have the right view of Jesus that your entire salvation depends on it. It is impossible to deny the Son and still have the Father and vice versa! To acknowledge the Son is to come into communion with the Father, for the Son is the only mediator of the Father. John says a similar thing in his second letter,

Whosoever transgresseth, and abides not in the doctrine of Christ, hath not God. He that abides in the doctrine of Christ, he hath both the Father and the Son. (II John 9.)

Let that therefore abide in you, which ye have heard from the beginning. If that which ye have heard from the beginning shall remain in you, ye also shall continue in the Son and the Father. And this is the promise that he hath promised us, even eternal life. (I John 2:24-25.)

Keep the original message, the simple Gospel, remain in it and allow it to remain in you. Recognise that the hunger for the new, the unique, this desire to innovate, comes out of a heart of unbelief and discontent! The original is none other than the teaching of the apostles. The promise of eternal life is linked to this loyalty to the apostolic teaching! "New and improved" Christian teachings can literally lead one to forfeit eternal life! This is extremely serious.

These things I have written unto you concerning them that seduce you. But the anointing which ye have received of Him abides in you, and you need not that any man teach you: but as the same anointing teaches you of all things, and is truth, and is no lie, and even as it hath taught you of all things, ye shall abide in him. (I John 2:26-27.)

The secret teachings and the supposed "new anointings" amount to denials of the sufficiency of Christ. I believe that the beloved apostle is basically saying, "They are trying to seduce you, they are telling you things that you want to hear! They make your new birth seem inadequate, you hunger for the 'new anointing' they imply that they have, you are tempted by the exciting new teachings they offer, but in order to receive these teachings and this anointing, you are in effect denying the adequacy of the original teachings (of the apostles), as well as the validity of the anointing all Christians receive when they are born again. Because the Holy Spirit abides in every single Christian, and leads and guides us into the Truth, you don't need these gurus or this 'new anointing'. Remain in the Gospel, abide in the anointing you have already received, and quit looking for that 'something else' Christ is adequate!"

And now little children, abide in Him; that when He shall appear, we may have confidence, and not be ashamed before him at His coming. If ye know that he is righteous, ye know that every one that doeth righteousness is born of Him. (I John 2:28-29.)

The return of our Lord and Saviour Jesus Christ, has a purifying effect, (see I John 3:3). Because we know that He is righteous, we can know that the ones who practice righteousness are the ones born of Him. This practice of righteousness is what will truly allow us confidence at His appearing. If we will remain in Him now, we will be able to confidently approach Him then!

I JOHN

CHAPTER 3

WHY LIVE RIGHT?

Behold what manner of love the Father has bestowed upon us, that we shall be called the sons of God: therefore the world knows us not, because it knew Him not. (I John 3:1.)

There are two things John declares which openly demonstrate the love of God to us: the sending of Jesus to die for us, and our adoption as children into sonship. The verse literally says "behold the foreign manner of love the Father has bestowed on us." Who else would take His enemies, save them at great personal expense, and then make them into His sons? What kind of love is this? The world cannot recognise us; after all, it didn't recognise His glory either: *"He was in the world, and the world was made by Him, yet, the world knew Him not" (John 1:10).* The same hostility the world showed Him, it will show us.

Beloved, now are we the sons of God, and it doth not appear what we shall be, but we know that when he shall appear, we shall be like Him; for we shall see Him as He is. (I John 3:2.)

Beloved (Greek: *agapetoi*), dearly loved by God, we know who we are now, Sons of God. We aren't searching for ourselves or trying to attain to any level, God has made us sons in His love.

As many as received Him, to them gave he the power to become sons of God, even to them who believe on His name, who were born not of blood or of the will of the flesh, or of the will of man, but of God. (John 1:12-13.)

On the other hand, our salvation is incomplete: *"It does not yet appear what we shall be."*

Whatever it is that we shall become, God shall accomplish it, not us. Seeing Christ will complete our salvation, for *"when we see Him we shall be like Him"*. Not through our efforts, not climbing the spiritual ladder, or obtaining secret teachings or new anointings, as the Gnostics. Seeing Jesus at His appearing is the means, becoming like Him – spirit, soul and body – is the end.

He that hath this hope in Him purifieth himself, even as He is pure. (I John 3:3.)

Whoever has this hope, (conformity to Christ, at His coming in glory, seeing Jesus as He truly is), finds that the hope itself has a purifying effect. It is already happening in part now, but at the parousia, the actual appearing of the Lord of Glory, all will be completed.

WHAT SIN IS, AND WHY CHRIST CAME

Whosoever committeth sin transgresseth the law: for sin is the transgression of the law. And ye know that he was manifested to take away our sins; and in Him is no sin. (I John 3:4-5.)

The Gnostics belittled the concept of sin, and at the same time promoted *antinomianism,* a christianised rejection of law in the name of a distorted grace. Law was irrelevant to them, and consequently sin was not regarded as a serious issue. Sin was seen as ignorance, not transgression, as the apostles taught. John would have us see that in both the Incarnation and the imminent return of Jesus, the defeat of the power and effects of sin is the central issue. We have already seen that the hope of the parousia is a purifying hope. Here the point is made that the reason Jesus came in the first place was to *"take away our sins"*. And how does the apostle define sin? *"Sin is lawlessness."* The very essence of sin is rebellion, breaking law, the law of God. Jesus never promoted an antinomianism, He came to take away the lawlessness in our hearts, to deal with the rebellion against the holy God of the Bible. There is no lawlessness in Him.

Whosoever abideth in Him sinneth not: whosoever sinneth hath not seen Him neither known Him. Little children let no man deceive you: he that doeth righteousness is righteous, even as He is righteous. (I John 3:6-7.)

John lays it out in a logical pattern. First of all, *"Sin is lawlessness"*. Secondly, the Son came into the world to *"take away our sins"*. The simple conclusion? Whoever remains in Him will not habitually practice lawlessness. If a man does habitually practice *iniquity* (lawlessness), he really doesn't know Jesus. Jesus has no lawlessness in Him.

He that committeth sin is of the devil; for the devil sinneth from the beginning. For this purpose was the Son of God manifested, that He might destroy the works of the devil. (I John 3:8.)

Another syllogism, making the same point.
1. Sin is of the Devil,
2. The Son of God came to destroy the works of the devil (which is sin, iniquity).
3. What does this make of the one who continues in lawlessness?

You figure it out! (See John 8:44,) The word for destroy, in verse 8, is a word that means to release. Obviously Satan's works have not been annihilated yet. The work of the Son of God has been to effect a release from Satan's cycle of iniquity for those who have been bound by it.

Whosoever is born of God doth not commit sin; for His seed remaineth in Him: and He cannot sin, because He is born of God. (I John 3:9.)

The false teachers of John's day, as well as ours, spiritualised righteousness, divorcing the concept from everyday life. They taught that all that really matters is who you are spiritually. The flesh to them was irrelevant, almost unreal. Therefore it would be possible to practice ungodliness, because your physical life is unessential. On the contrary those really born of God, cannot habitually practice sin; the seed of God, (James 1:18) remains in us and it is that very life that condemns sin! Therefore we cannot practice sin with impunity!

John Stott does an excellent summary of this in his Tyndale New Testament commentary:

If then the whole purpose of Christ's first appearing was to remove sins and to undo the works of the devil, Christians must not compromise with either sin or the Devil, or they will find themselves fighting against Christ. If the first step to holiness is to recognise the sinfulness of sin, both in its essence as lawlessness and in its diabolical origin, the second step is to see its absolute incompatibility with Christ in his sinless person and his saving work. The more clearly we grasp these facts, the more incongruous sin will appear, and the more determined we shall be to be rid of it.

(Stott, *Letters of John*, Tyndale NT Commentaries, Eerdmans, p.129.)

In this the children of God are manifest, and the children of the devil; whosoever doeth not righteousness is not of God, neither he that loveth not His brother. (I John 3:10.)

It is obvious, but because of the confusion of the issues and the pseudo-spirituality, the false anointings and the antinomianism, the obvious needs to be restated. Those who don't habitually practice righteousness are not of God, they are of the Devil. Righteousness, love and truth all interweave, the one cannot be obtained without the other. Thus John moves naturally from the subject of righteousness/unrighteousness, into an examination of the invalidity of a Christian confession while harbouring hatred.

OF LOVE AND HATRED

For this is the message ye have heard from the beginning, that we should love one another. Not as Cain, who was of that wicked One, and slew His brother. And wherefore slew He him? Because his own works were evil and his brothers righteous. (I John 3:11-12.)

Not only is sin *"of the devil"*, so is hatred and murder. Holiness is impossible without love, and love is not lawlessness. Both lawlessness and hatred come from the same source: the devil. Cain literally hated his brother for being good! Because Cain himself didn't abide in the truth, he compromised with the evil one, and abode in the darkness of hatred, and killed his brother for being righteous!

Marvel not, my brethren, if the world hate you. We know that we have passed from death unto life, because we love the brethren. He that loveth not his brother abideth in death. (I John 3:13-14.)

Cain is like the world. The world also is hostile to God, and would seek its own way to God. As Cain did, the world offers to God the works of its own hand, the sweat of its brow as a sacrifice, anything but the broken, bloody lamb! As Cain hated Abel, the world hates us. Whoever hates is in darkness, like Cain and the world. One of the marks of a Christian is a love for the brethren. Those who say, "I am a Christian and I love God but I don't want anything to do with the church", are liars. They remain in death.

Whoever hates his brother is a murderer: and ye know that no murderer hath eternal life abiding in Him. (I John 3:15.)

As the practice of sin and the claim of righteousness is a contradiction, so is the practice of hatred and the confidence of eternal life. The two are mutually exclusive. Anyone that can hate a brother, or who seeks to diminish a Christian, is not saved. If a person rejoices in the downfall of a believer, and does not rather mourn; if one hates the success, and grieves over the favour of another Christian, one cannot possibly have eternal life; such a person is more like Cain and the world than he is a Christian. Christ is so bound up in the church, that to hate a Christian is to hate Christ; particularly if that hatred is provoked because of the goodness of the Christian!

Hereby we perceive the love of God, because he laid down His life for us: and we ought to lay down our lives for the brethren. But whoso hath this world's goods and seeth his brother have need, and shutteth up his bowels of compassion from him, how dwelleth the love of God in Him? (I John 3:16-17.)

As they did with righteousness, the Gnostics spiritualised love also, thus allowing for a professing Christian to claim some kind of higher kind of love for God, whilst at the same time and without conscience showing utter spite and contempt for other Christians. (The same thing is occurring these days.) What does it mean to love God? *"If you love me, keep my commandments."* What does it mean to love man? *"To lay down our lives for the brethren."* It is a concrete love, an incarnate love, a willingness to put aside my own interests, preferences, and pride, and be willing to serve the interests of my Christian brothers, to stick with them, and to allow them to stick with me. Only by this practice can we truly perceive the love of God.

My little children, let us not love in word, neither in tongue, but in deed and in truth. (I John 3:18.)

CALMING YOUR UNASSURED HEART

And hereby we know that we are of the truth, and shall assure our hearts before Him. For if our heart condemn us, God is greater than our hearts and knoweth all things. Beloved, if our hearts condemn us not, than have we confidence before God. (I John 3:19-21.)

The self-knowledge, that you have truly loved *"in deed and in truth"*, is particularly essential in times of self doubt. John presents the love walk, as the way to know *"that we are of the truth"*, in the context of assuring our hearts before Him. In other words, if you can honestly say to yourself, with a clear conscience, that you are a loving, self-sacrificing person because of Jesus Christ, this will go a long way toward calming your heart in times of doubt. The word "condemn" is the Greek *katagnoskein*, which is a compound word *kata*, "against", and the word *gnoskein*, "to know". Does your heart refuse to be comforted, knowing something against you? Remember I John 1:9. Remember that God is greater, more merciful, willing to forgive and restore, than even your own heart! You may as well confess because God also *"knows all thing"*s. Either your knowledge that you have walked in love because of Jesus will comfort and calm your heart before God, or God's knowledge of all things, and your open confession before Him who is truly greater than our hearts, will bring assurance before God.

Beloved, if our heart condemn us not, then have we confidence before God. And whatsoever we ask we receive of Him, because we keep His commandments, and do those things that are pleasing in His sight. (I John 3:21-22.)

Blessed are you if your heart doesn't know anything against yourself! Confidence before God is a blessing; to be without it should lead us to serious seeking and prayer. Answered prayer is the way God honours a clean conscience. A clear conscience should be a high priority in our life; when prayers are not answered that should not be considered normal, but in itself a matter for prayer.

And this is His commandment, that we should believe on the name of his Son, Jesus Christ, and love one another, as he gave us commandment. And he that keepeth his commandments dwelleth in him and he in him. And hereby we know that he abideth in us, by the Spirit which he hath given us. (I John 3:23-24.)

All righteousness, love and assurance come as a result of keeping this one commandment to believe on the name (the entire person; all He says, all He stands for, what He did and who he is) of the Son of God, Jesus Christ, and consequently, to love one another. By keeping this commandment we remain in Him, and he in us (see John 14:21) through the Spirit, who prompts us inwardly to love, to do right and to hate wrong.

I JOHN

CHAPTER 4

Beloved, believe not every spirit, but try the spirits, whether they are of God: because many false prophets have gone out into the world. (I John 4:1.)

Test the spirits, John cautions us; don't just accept every prophecy, apostle, "word" or movement that comes along; think critically. The word for test in Greek is *dokimazein,* which means to think or examine. The word for spirit is *pneuma,* which means wind. In other words, test every spiritual thing critically; every influence, minister, teaching and prophecy; evaluate them all in the light of the Word of truth, as well as in the light and the love of God. Why? *"Because many false prophets have gone out into the world."*

Hereby know ye the Spirit of God: Every spirit that confesseth that Jesus Christ has come in the flesh is of God: And every spirit that confesseth not that Jesus Christ is come in the flesh is not of God: and this is that spirit of antichrist, whereof ye have heard that it should come; and even now already is it in the world. (I John 4:2-3.)

Here is how you can recognise the Spirit of Go: when the consistent teaching is that Jesus Christ has come and remains in the flesh. This is not a one-sentence shibboleth, some kind of a litmus test. Any spirit or false teacher can mouth the confession, "Jesus Christ came in the flesh", and then go on to deny this truth by consistently teaching to the contrary. The spirit of anti-christ always ends up distorting this truth of the full humanity and full deity of Jesus Christ in some fashion. The phrase *"has come"*, is *elelythota* in Greek, which is in the perfect tense and means, "has come and remains". The modern emphasis among Pentecostals and Charismatics on following the "anointing", singing to it, even making pilgrimages to it, seems to be an application of this scripture. Here we have a christ (i.e. anointing) which is being sought and worshipped and travelled to, but is not incarnate. A new anointing is a new christ! The anti-christ spirit would spiritualise Christ, it would make a distinction between the person Jesus, and the Christ, setting the world up for the anti-christ!

YOU, THEY AND WE

Ye are of God, little children, and have overcome them: because greater is he that is in you, than he that is in the world. (I John 4:4.)

In verses 4-6, John refers to three groups, "You, They and We". "You", refers to those faithful to the Father and the Son, and to the doctrine of Christ; those who have not accepted the "spiritualised Christ", who have not bought into the Gnostic "new thing". You have overcome the false teaching which amounts to a spiritualised distortion of the person of Jesus Christ, and a departure from God's light (holiness and openness) and God's love (in the context of His law). You have overcome this by Him that is within you, that is by the indwelling Christ, who through His Spirit bears witness to the truth. Obviously, He is greater than the one who abides in the world (Satan, the adversary, the spirit of error).

They are of the world: therefore speak they of the world, and the world heareth them. (I John 4:5.)

They? Who are referred to as "They"? They are the ones who, though they were once among us, came out of us because they were not really of us (see I John 2:19). They are those who would change Christianity, who would spiritualise Christ, or divide Jesus from Christ in some way. Because of their doctrinal unfaithfulness, their confession of Christ is belied by their unholy and unloving lives. Because they don't really embrace the Christ as having "come and remained in" the flesh, their own spirituality is spectral, mystical, lawless and loveless. Their prophecies and teachings find a ready audience, however, because those who are of the world readily receive these ones. The world, that whole of society which seeks to establish life which is independent of the God of the Bible, can appreciate Gnosticism, it can readily receive the "Manifested Sons of God" teachings, New Thought, New Age, or any of the other countless distortions of Christianity which exalt the self, instead of putting it in the place of submission to a holy God.

We are of God: he that knoweth God heareth us; he that is not of God heareth not us. Hereby know ye the spirit of truth, and the spirit of error. (I John 4:6.)

We know who "they" are, as well as who "You" refers to. We now come to "We". To whom does the apostle refer? This "We" is important. They become a measuring line as to who is of God and who isn't. Knowing who they are and people's reactions to them can mean knowing the difference between the "Spirit of truth and the spirit of error"! The answer is that "We" are the apostles who gave us the New Testament. Whoever doesn't care what the apostles taught on any given subject, or who would distort the teachings of the apostles, or who won't hear the apostles, or would seek to supersede the teachings of the apostles with "New Revelation" is not of God. Ours is an apostolic faith. Any teacher who feels he is beyond the apostles is a false one.

THE PRIMACY OF LOVE

Beloved, let us love one another: for love is of God; and every one that loveth is born of God, and knoweth God. He that loveth not knoweth not God; for God is love. (I John 4:7-8.)

Truth, light (holiness), and love: these are the marks of authentic Christianity. Therefore John's Epistle continuously revolves around these three. The concept of Christianity is reciprocal love: *"Beloved . . . love one another."* Because we have been and are the objects of God's free and undeserved love, our response should be to love. The Greek opening of this sentence is *"Agapetoi agapomen".* We who are the recipients of *Agape* – God's undeserved, self sacrificing love – should in response, *"agape* one another"; love each other in a self-sacrificing, undeserved pursuit of the good of one another.

Why should Christians love? Because we ourselves have been loved by God, freely. He has saved us and made us acceptable to Himself while we were yet His enemies! *"Love is of God."* We should love because love comes from our God, it reflects His very character. *"God is love."* He doesn't have love, He is love! Love is the very essence of the nature of God. Love marks and permeates everything God does. God loves, He gives, and forgives, even to his enemies and to the undeserving. Because *"God is love"* those who are born of God and know Him in truth, love as a result.

In this was manifested the love of God toward us, because that God sent His only begotten Son into the world, that we might live through Him. Herein is love, not that we loved God, but that He loved us, and sent his Son to be the propitiation for our sins. (I John 4:9-10.)

94

Our loving one another is a result of the initiative God took in loving us. This love is not esoteric; it is concrete, rooted in space and time. God's love has been manifested by the incarnation, culminating in the cross. It is literally love in the flesh! He gave us his *monogenes*, His only unique and precious Son. If you had run your hand up the side of the cross, you would soon have a handful of splinters! They had to embalm his body. They wrapped him in graveclothes. He was crucified *under Pontius Pilate* – there was a Governor, an administration. It was on a specific date, at a specific place that God manifested His love. Those who search for manifestations of God's love ("if God loves me He will fill my mouth with gold fillings, or slay me in the spirit") are guilty of unbelief. God has commended His love to us, when He sent His Son in history and space to be an offering for our sins.

"Beloved if God so loved us we ought also to love one another. No man hath seen God at any time. If we love one another, God dwelleth in us, and His love is perfected in us" (1 John 4:11-12)

Our love for each other should come out of this. We who know the cross, have no choice but to seek each other's well-being, to turn away from self-seeking, in the light of this tremendous love. No one can see God in this world, but because God is love, when those who have been loved by God begin to love each other as a result, and when they love each other in a concrete and practical way (as God has loved us), then the world can see the unseen God dwelling in us! The discerning can see God in the cross of Jesus, and the discerning can also see God in the love of the church. As we practise this reciprocal love, it is perfected, matured in us. The love of God in the church is something that we are to grow and develop in, unto maturity.

HE DWELLS IN US, WE DWELL IN HIM

Hereby know we that we dwell in him, and he in us, because he has given us of his Spirit. (I John 4:13)

The Spirit is the subjective aspect of our assurance. How do we know that we dwell in Him and He in us? The Spirit. How do we recognise the Spirit? It is the Spirit that makes us want to love, that moves us to aspire to obedience, that causes us to be willing to justify God, that resonates within us to the teachings of the apostles. I never had these attributes until the Spirit came.

And we have seen and do testify that the Father sent the Son to be the saviour of the world. Whosoever shall confess that Jesus is the Son of God, God dwelleth in Him and He in God. (I John 4:14-15.)

The Spirit testifies to our hearts of the Gospel, and so do the apostles. *"We have seen and do testify . . ."* It is the twofold testimony, of the Word and the Spirit, the objective and the subjective, which assures our hearts that we know God. God dwells in those who are moved by this twofold testimony to confess Jesus, to live in the light, and to abide in love. The Father (because of love) sent the Son (Jesus Christ, come in the flesh) to be the Saviour of the world, the propitiation for our sins (assuming you are willing to confess those sins in the light of God, who is Light).

And we have known and believed the love that God hath to us. God is love; and he that dwelleth in love dwelleth in God, and God in him. (I John 4:16.)

Who can really love, and who can remain in love? Those who have known and believed the testimony of the Father and the Son.

CONFIDENCE IN THE DAY OF CRISIS

Herein is our love made perfect, that we may have boldness in the day of judgment: because as He is, so are we in this world. (I John 4:17.)

Love "perfected" refers not to God's love toward us, but to our development in that love, expressing it to others. The Greek word for confidence, is *parresia*, which means boldness, openness, even freedom of speech. God's love, as revealed in the incarnation of Jesus Christ and ministered by the Holy Spirit towards the one who truly *"knows and believes"* in it, breeds confidence, particularly in the light of His coming (I John 2:28), and of the coming *crisis*, which is the day of judgment. To the extent that we love in this world as He has shown us, *"we have boldness in the day of crisis."*.

There is no fear in love; but perfect love casts out fear: because fear has torment. He that feareth is not made perfect in love. We love Him because He first loved us. (I John 4:18-19.)

God has already loved me at my very worst; He has seen me completely in His holy light, and still loved me. *"Fear has to do with 'kolasis' (punishment)"*, is the literal clause. Fear itself is the down-payment of the coming punishment. Perfecting love, and the accompanying confidence towards God, is the down-payment of the coming glory.

In two ways we have known and believed in the love God has shown to us: objectively and subjectively. Objectively in the incarnation and death of Jesus, and subjectively through the Spirit. We are God's children; we have been forgiven; we want this for everyone else we know. We seek their good because of Jesus. We know we are not destined for punishment. This has a profound psychological effect on those who truly believe this. The beautiful thing is that this is not something we

97

had to initiate and keep going: our love is a response to His; *We love Him, because He first loved us.* This is liberating.

John has addressed the past, the present and the future in the light of the love of God. God has shown us his love, He has commended it to us in the self-giving of His only unique Son. Love is based upon a concrete action of God. Presently *"we know and believe the love God has towards us"*, we have the Spirit, and the ability and command to show that love, to develop it, to grow in it together as we lay down our lives for one another. This affects the future, in particular two future events, which for the ungodly and the sinner, ought to strike terror: the coming of our Lord and the *crisis*, the coming judgment. This love of God, that he has revealed in history and that he has mediated to us through the Word and the Spirit and which we are to cultivate in common life together, has the effect of giving us boldness as we approach the future. We aren't under wrath we are the children of God. God is our loving Father, *As Jesus was, so are we in this world.*

If a man say, I love God, and hateth his brother, he is a liar: for he that loveth not his brother whom he hath seen, how can he love God whom he hath not seen. And this commandment have we from him, that he who loveth God love his brother also. (I John 4:20-21.)

As always, John insists not upon idealised, spiritualised love, but actual, concrete love. After all, *"Jesus Christ has come in the flesh"*. John's formula, *"If a man say . . . but . . ."*, is repeated here on the issue of love, as it was earlier on the issue of light (I John 1:6-10), and truth (I John 2:22-23). Who lies? The one who claims to love God but hates his brother. The Gnostic lives in the idealised world, "up in the heavenly places", a world that is about self-improvement, self-discovery. He is caught up in his love for God, which is more *eros* love than the genuine love, demonstrated by the laying down of Jesus' life for others! Those who

98

have truly known the love of the God of the Bible are compelled by that love to imitate it in practical ways, not up in the heavenlies, but here on earth in loving our own brothers and sisters. Anything "higher" is a delusion. No one has excelled beyond the commandment to love his brother.

I JOHN

CHAPTER 5

Whosoever believeth that Jesus is the Christ is born of God: and every one that loveth him that begat loveth him also that is begotten of him. (I John 5:1.)

Believing in the doctrine of Christ, and persevering in that belief is here presented by John as evidence of having been "born of God". So is loving Christians. John has already pointed out the incongruity of claiming to love the unseen God of the Bible while at the same time hating another Christian. Here he states it positively. Everyone who has been born of the Father and loves Him, will as a consequence love all those who have also been born of the Father.

By this we know that we love the children of God, when we love God, and keep His commandments. (I John 5:2.)

How is this love to be measured? How do we know we love the children of God? Loving the children of God is impossible without truly loving God. Only a born-again Christian can truly love born-again Christians. How do we know whether we love God or not? Those who love God in truth, love other Christians and will want to keep His commandments (echoes of John 14:15, 21).

For this is the love of God, that we keep His commandments: and his commandments are not grievous. (I John 5:3.)

Love is not lawlessness. The essence of the love of God is not a mere emotional experience, rather, as in a marriage, loving God includes a moral commitment. I love the One who saved me, I want to love Him after His own terms, after His commandments.

The commandments of God are neither the means of salvation, nor meaningless do's and don'ts: they are the measure and teaching of concrete love for God. Once they were grievous to me, when I was his enemy, in rebellion to His loving rule. But now that which was once unbearable to me, I delight in! What changed? Not the commandments of God, but I have changed! Through the new birth of the Spirit, we now want to be taught of God, we want to love as he has commanded, this is another major sign of genuine Christianity. False spirituality, such as Gnosticism, is either legalistic, or antinomian. True spirituality is a change of heart, a loving response to saving grace.

For whatsoever is born of God overcomes the world: and this is the victory that overcometh the world, even our faith. (I John 5:4.)

As I stated above, the change is within us. That which is of the world, the fallen values of the whole of human culture which seeks to live life independently of the God of the Bible, has been overcome through the new birth. We are no longer of the world; we no longer see things the way we once did: our values have changed. Adam and Eve were the ones who launched the world system which has developed in opposition to Christ, when they prayed in effect, "Not Thy Will be done, but mine be done"! They, as created beings, exchanged their place as worshippers, made in the image of God, for the lie that they could in fact make their own judgments, pave their own ways, decide for themselves the meaning of good and evil, that they might be *"as gods"*. In the process, they trampled commitment, gratitude and loyalty to God under foot, and the world system came into being. But Jesus overcame the world, by praying *"Not my will, but thine be done"*. He who was indeed God (and is) *"did not regard equality with God a thing to be grasped."* (Philippians 2), He humbled himself, letting go of self, and in that submission to the Father to the point of death He prevailed over the fallen values of this bankrupt world.

Who is he that overcometh the world, but he that believeth that Jesus is the Son of God? (I John 5:5.)

It is being born again that empowers us to hold to the truth as revealed in Jesus, that Jesus is the Christ, the Son of God come into the world as man to save us. This is the belief that contradicts the central belief of the world system opposed to the Father and the Son, that is, the idea that man can save himself, that we can ascend up to God's level, that we don't need a condescending God to save us. Worldliness is not external, therefore it cannot be overcome by external means. Worldliness is a belief system which permeates everything else, therefore it can only be supplanted, overcome, by a superior belief. Man cannot rise up, he cannot save himself, he is too bankrupt and helpless. God had to descend, Jesus Christ had to come in the flesh to redeem fallen humanity. This is the faith that overcomes the world.

THE THREEFOLD TESTIMONY

This is he that came by water and by blood, even Jesus Christ: not by water only, but by water and blood. And it is the Spirit that beareth witness, because the Spirit is Truth. (I John 5:6.)

The apostle takes pains to be particular about exactly which Jesus he refers to, for there are many false concepts of Jesus. He seems to be refuting an oft-repeated error called Adoptionism. This is the Christological error which teaches that Jesus of Nazareth became Christ at His baptism (by water). When the Father spoke from heaven, affirming *"This is my Son in whom I am well pleased"*, at this point Jesus was adopted by the Father, and "enchristed". But the adoptionistic error also teaches that when Jesus was crucified (by blood), the Christ-spirit lifted from Him, rendering Him a mortal man again. The implications of this error are far-reaching. For example, they would render Jesus to be nothing more than a mere man anointed by the Spirit. The conclusion would be that if Jesus could be anointed by the Spirit, so could any other man. This is not far removed from the teachings of Kenneth Copeland and Kenneth Hagin. Hagin asserts that the believer is "Just as much an incarnation as Jesus of Nazareth was." Copeland is even bolder, claiming that if he had had the revelation knowledge that Jesus had, he too could have died on the cross and "whipped Satan".

John affirms that Jesus was the Christ when He came into the world, when he went to be baptised, and when he died on the cros, and rose again by the Spirit of Holiness, and He is at this time the Christ of God, in the flesh: *"This is he . . ."* Pentecost did not come about because an ordinary man became "Christ" for three years and then ceased being Christ at his death. Pentecost happened because God became a man; He came to us in the flesh, identified with us in our humanity and sinful condition (water), then, as God in the flesh, subjected Himself to an ignoble death (blood) as a sacrifice for our sins. Only after the resurrection and ascension occurred could there be an outpouring of the Spirit. The Spirit testifies to the One who came by water and by blood!

For there are three that bear record in heaven, the Father, the Word, and the Holy Ghost: and these three are One. (I John 5:7.)

There is much controversy concerning this strong Trinitarian confession. But what can we do except embrace all of Scripture? I am not prepared to take out scissors and start cutting and pasting the bible. By the mouth of two or three witnesses let everything be confirmed! The record is the testimony of Christ. The Father certainly has born witness to it countless times, but in the context, at Jesus' baptism the Father spoke out, *"This is my beloved Son in whom I am well pleased."* The Son, in this place fittingly referred to as the Word, also testifies Jesus is the Word of God, he fulfilled all of the prophecies, he met all of the standards that the Word testified that the Christ of God should meet. Certainly the Spirit has testified of the reality of Jesus Christ, God come in the flesh, and does yet testify.

And there are three that bear witness in earth, the spirit, and the water, and the blood: and these three are one. (I John 5:8.)

There is an earthly testimony as well to Jesus Christ. The new Spirit whom God gives to men who believe, which cries out "Abba Father!", and the witnessing community, the church, through baptism and communion, offer continual testimony to Jesus Christ as having come and having remained in the flesh.

If we receive the witness of men, the witness of God is greater: For this is the witness of God which he hath testified of His Son. (I John 5:9.)

At Jesus' trial, witnesses who contradicted one another were accepted and Jesus was condemned. But here we have the powerful witness of God, both the heavenly witness and the earthly. The Father testifies to the Son; He speaks out of the heavens, affirming Him; He raises Him up from the grave! The Word testifies to the Son of God, for before He came in the flesh numerous and multiple prophecies described in detail events in his life that it would be impossible to predict, unless you were God. This is the One that the prophets foretold. The Spirit testifies to the Son, for after His ascension, the Spirit was poured out upon all flesh, and the Spirit bears witness to people of all times and walks of life, that Jesus is the Christ. On earth the church bears witness by the new Spirit; those who had at one time been thieves, become givers; those who were immoral become virginal; those who were selfish become missionaries and martyrs. The church has born continuous testimony through two thousand years of baptisms, preaching, communion and martyrdom. This comprises the testimony of God!

He that believeth on the Son of God hath the witness in himself: he that believeth not God hath made Him a liar; because he believeth not the record God gave of His Son. (I John 5:10.)

In the light of the testimony of God, unbelief becomes a moral issue. Whoever accepts this testimony is given deeper assurance yet. Whoever rejects it is making God out to be a liar, which is a serious sin. To not believe in Jesus is not an understandable weakness, it is a serious sin. God has clearly testified to His Son; there can be no excuse for unbelief!

And this is the record, that God hath given to us eternal life, and this life is in his Son. He that hath the Son has the life, and he that hath not the Son of God has not the life. (I John 5:11-12.)

He that believes God, He that accepts the testimony, he that believes that Jesus is the Son of God, and he that hath the Son are all ways of saying the same thing: whoever accepts Jesus Christ as Lord and Saviour. The blessing of accepting the testimony of God is this: eternal life. That life is found only in Jesus, who literally is *"The way, the truth and the life."* We are told that we who have the Son have this life, it is a present possession, a new kind of life from the Father. Whoever denies the Son does not have this life. It is a gift, the result of the incarnation, death and resurrection of the Son, it is this life that makes us able to be sons of God ourselves.

These things have I written unto you that believe on the name of the Son of God; that you may know that you have eternal life, and that you may believe on the name of the Son of God. (I John 5:13.)

These people had been confused about who they were and what they had in Jesus. The false teachers and Gnostics blew them away with their pseudo-spirituality, their visions, revelations and levels of development. This letter was written to let us know that we have as a present possession eternal life. Not as some attainment ahead but a gift through simply believing on the name (person, saying, works, character) of the Son of God, and to encourage and allow us to continue believing on that name. This letter is full of assurance: you can know that you are saved and will go to heaven!

CONFIDENCE IN PRAYER

And this is the confidence that we have in him, that if we ask anything according to His will he heareth us: and if we know He heareth us, whatsoever we ask, we know we have the petitions we have desired of Him. (I John 5:14-15.)

The confidence of eternal life is accompanied by confidence of answered prayer. Eternal life means being brought back into communion with God. The word for confidence *parresia* can also be translated *freedom of speech*. We who believe the testimony of God concerning His Son, can come to God and expect an audience. We can tell Him what we need, we can pray and expect answers to prayer. Eternal life is now as well as in the future. To know that your Father has heard your petitions is to know that He will answer you.

If any man see a brother sin a sin which is not unto death, he shall ask, and He shall give him life for them that sin not unto death. There is a sin unto death: I do not say that he shall pray for it. All unrighteousness is sin: and there is a sin not unto death. (I John 5:16-17.)

Take, for example, the case of a brother who has fallen into sin; how does our confident access to the Father apply here? John assures us that if we ask, the Lord will surely give us life for those who have sinned (sin leads to death). But John doesn't advise prayer for those who sin the sin unto death (which, according to the context, would be apostatising from the confession that *"Jesus Christ has come and remains in the flesh"*).

The distortion and rejection of the doctrine of Christ is certainly a sin unto spiritual death, but all John says is that he isn't saying we should pray for them. All sins are odious to God, because they are all unjust, but God does forgive and restore in answer to the prayers of His children.

SUMMARY

We know that whosoever is born of God sinneth not; but he that is begotten of God keepeth himself, and that wicked One toucheth him not. (I John 5:18.)

John now summarises the entire letter, with three "We know's . . .". The first concerns the true believer's relationship to sin, "Whoever is born of God does not persistently sin." Through the seed of God, through the eternal life, the child of God is kept from the power of sin, and from the wicked One.

And we know that we are of God, and the whole world lieth in wickedness. (I John 5:19.)

We also know that there is a difference between we who believe in the doctrine of Christ and the whole world. It is a difference of origin. We are children begotten of God. He is our source of life, we are to reflect His light, His love and above all else, His Son. On the other hand, the whole world lies in the wicked One — and the idea here is that of Samson lying in the arms of Delilah. Not extremist pockets of an otherwise benign world, but the whole world. Jesus referred to Satan as the prince of this world; Paul called him the "god of this age".

And we know that the Son of God is come, and hath given us an understanding, that we may know him that is true, and we are in him that is true, even in His Son, Jesus Christ. This is the true God and eternal life. (I John 5:20.)

Finally, we are the true "knowing ones", not the Gnostics. What is it that we know? We know, objectively, that the Son of God has come into the world, into history, in the flesh, to redeem us. Only this incarnation could make us sons of God and deliver us from the wicked One. By His coming from above, and our faith in His coming, we are delivered from the bankrupt and man-exalting values of this passing world. He has given to us an understanding – an understanding that is subjective as well. We now know Him that is true, indeed we are *in* Him that is true, Jesus Christ, the Son of the living God. The God of the Jesus who came in the flesh is the true God, only He is eternal life. Notice the intellectual aspect of this verse, *"We know . . . an understanding . . . knowing Him . . . true God".*

The true God is not anti-rational, He has given us an understanding.

Little children, keep yourself from idols. (I John 5:20.)

Idols do not have to mean other Gods. John writes his final word to the *"little children"* of the church. In this case idols must of necessity refer to the distortions of the person of Christ. The dis-incarnate, spiritualised Christ of the Gnostics is an idol and incapable of giving eternal life. So is the "new anointing" of today. The Jesus of liberal Christianity is an idol also. The idols Christians must guard themselves from are not Zeus or Apollo, but rather distorted images of the Jesus Christ of Scripture, who came to us in the flesh. Knowing Him alone is eternal life (John 17:3).

EPILOGUE

IMPLICATIONS OF THE NEW ANOINTING

If there has been one distinguishing characteristic of popular Charismatic, Pentecostal and even Evangelical Christianity at the turn of this millennium, it has been the pursuit of the "New Thing", the "great endtimes revival" which would sweep the world into the Kingdom and usher in the "greatest move of God ever seen", greater even than in the book of the Acts. Through the prophecies and teachings of Charismatic leaders, an expectation has developed of a last days cutting edged church, moving in such power and anointing that world leaders would search out the wisdom of our leaders and whole nations would fall trembling at their feet! In spite of the fact that there is no scriptural justification for this fantasy, it appeals to the desire in a good many Christians to be seen as relevant and powerful. Millions around the world have bought into it, as evidenced by the immediate pilgrimages to such sites as Toronto, Pensacola and many other lesser locations designated as having received the "New Anointing".

In three years estimates of up to a half million people visited Toronto Airport Vineyard, and stood in lines at times for three and four hours waiting to come into the church! And for what were they waiting? Not for the preaching and teaching of the Word of God, as much as for an experience with the "presence of the Lord"! Such experiences ranged from uncontrollable laughter, to guttural roaring, crying, prophesying, being slain in the spirit, put into trances, and even for many, being put into such an altered state of consciousness, they made animal noises! It was not the Word of the Lord as much as an unmediated experience of "the presence" of the Lord which the pilgrims sought.

To their credit, the Assemblies of God initially resisted this excess, having seen it all before in the "New Order of the Latter Rain" movement which they had denounced as heretical in 1950. At one point, they could see plainly that the Vineyard movement, out of which the Toronto Phenomenon grew, was influenced by the very Latter Rain/Manifested Sons of God errors that they once refuted. They were particularly cautious of the Kansas City Prophets of the Vineyard. Unfortunately, it was only a matter of time before an Assemblies of God version of the Toronto Blessing sprang forth at the Brownsville Assembly of God in Pensacola, Florida. That particular outpouring became the turning point that brought the bulk of the Assemblies of God movement into what became known as "The River".

In spite of protestations to the contrary, the Assembly of God version of the "New Anointing" is identical to the Vineyard's version. This is because, rather than coming down out of heaven as a "Rushing, mighty wind", Steve Hill brought this "New Anointing" over from England, after asking his hosts, "Where is the Holy Spirit moving in London?" and being directed to the Holy Trinity church, Brompton, and having hands laid upon him by the vicar, Sandy Millar. (HTB is nearly synonymous with the Toronto Blessing in the British mind, having done more than anyone to blanket the churches in the UK with it. In fact the expression Toronto Blessing was coined by an HTB staff member.) Steve brought "it" home, where he ministered "it" to the Brownsville Assembly of God in Pensacola, Florida, where perhaps another million have gone to get "it" and to take "it" back to their own churches. In this way what was once primarily a Vineyard, and then a Charismatic, phenomenon, has been brought into the mainstream of classical Pentecostalism and even the wider evangelical world.

A prominent example within the Assemblies of God of a pastor and church radicalised by this "New Anointing", comes out of the testimony of Pastor Steve Benson, from 1st Assembly of God in Grand Rapids, Michigan. Here is his own account of his initial encounter with this "New Anointing",

When Steve [Hill] and John [Kilpatrick] started to anoint me with oil, they doubled over and shouted, 'The Anointing!!' I collapsed. I felt like the three of us were swirling around the room like a vortex of a whirlpool . . . they walked out of the office. I felt as if my body was being pulled apart . . . was being stretched out of shape beyond measure. I asked the Lord, 'What does this mean, Lord?' The Lord answered, 'I'm just crucifying your flesh'. I opened my eyes and the first thing I looked at were my hands, because they were tingling with the power of God.

The manifestations of this spirit, as you can see, go far beyond the commonly understood gifts of the Spirit. This is not about speaking in tongues, or even very much about prophecy or divine healing. The manifestation of this "New Anointing" is more likely to bring people into an unmediated experience of power. Joseph Chambers' *End Times Digest*, March 1997, quotes Pastor John Kilpatrick, of the Brownsville Assembly of God, as testifying,

I have hundreds of times laid hands on the unsaved and I have watched them being thrown across the ground. I mean I have watched them fly through the air, fall to the ground to where they couldn't get up again for an hour or two hours. The next thing you know is, "What shall I do to be saved?" . . . Friends, I am not talking hundreds anymore, thousands this has happened to. Thousands have been convinced by the power . . . We have had people, agnostics and God haters, businessmen coming into our meetings and they have been thrown into the air up against a wall and hit the ground when we shook their hand.

112

What are we to make of this "New Anointing"? Is this the Holy Spirit of God doing a "new thing" among us? Or could this be something fleshly and human, or perhaps even something more sinister? Since the mid 1990s when the Assemblies of God mainstreamed it "The River" of blessing, this "presence" that people have been willing to embark on pilgrimages to various locations, has swollen into a floodtide of unusual manifestations and experiences! No longer just in Toronto or Pensacola, hundreds and even thousands of churches are reporting their own manifestations of this "Presence". Here is just a sampling of New Wine testimonies reported on the Internet:

Automatic finger pointing - *"It was prophesied over me that I was a weathervane . . . all of a sudden my finger started pointing at people and in the air towards heaven . . . I was in a very conservative church and during the service, there went my finger. I sat there for a half an hour that way . . . The Pastor got up to give the altar call for those to get saved. He was so drunk in the spirit he could not. He then called another pastor forward to give the altar call. He also fell laughing to the floor. The first pastor managed to pull himself to the podium still laughing and said. 'If you want to get saved, see that ladies finger, follow that finger . . .'"*

Brave Heart anointing? – *"That night the place [Churc] was full with two thousand plus persons, and there was a real spirit of anticipation . . . Pastor ----- got up . . . as he began to exhort the people during the announcements, he took hold of the large Brave Heart sword that was there from the night before. He began to get bolder and bolder as he pointed the sword towards the congregation, and charged them to a revived spirit . . . after two hours . . . [he] suggested the whole church 'Pass under the sword through a fire tunnel.' The two senior Pastors . . . would hold up two swords, so as to form an arch . . . all two thousand of the congregation waited patiently for the chance to be prayed through the fire tunnel."*

Starting out in the flesh – *"She recounted her experiences in 'coming into the river' during a Rodney Howard Browne meeting at a church across town [Marilyn Hickey's church] . . . She had a very tough time figuring out what God wanted from her, and she*

really wanted to get into the laughing thing. God told her to yield. 'Whaddya mean, yield?' .
. . she was flat on her back and God told her to start laughing even if it was 'just the flesh'
to start out with. In a few minutes something rose up inside her and away she went. The
point being, she had given God something to work with . . ."

I didn't really have to try very hard to find these testimonies, they are a mere skimming of a bulging file, gleaned from testimonies from the Internet, *Charisma* magazine, and other sources of the manifestations of this "New Anointing". In fact I deliberately didn't use some of the more extreme manifestations, the above are just typical ones, so as to not sensationalise. I haven't gotten into the multiple gold dust secretions, "birthings", and oil and even feathers that are allegedly supernaturally manifesting in countless "renewal" churches and gatherings. We are obviously no longer awaiting this "New Anointing" it is here and people are being impacted by it. This is why I believe that we should consider this anointing in the light of several truths.

First of all Jesus warned us specifically when he cautioned,

Then if any man say unto you, Lo, here is Christ, or there, believe it not. For there shall arise false Christs, and false prophets and shall show great signs and wonders; insomuch if it be possible they shall deceive the very elect [and by the Greek construction, it is clear that Jesus is saying it is possible] *. . . Wherefore if they shall say unto you, Behold he is in the desert; go not forth: behold he is in the secret chambers; believe it not. (Matthew 24:23-26.)*

Note that the warning does not concern the problem of people claiming that Jesus is here or there, but that Christ is! This is a very significant distinction, because no one is claiming that Jesus has come to Pensacola or Toronto, or to one of Rodney Howard Browne's crusades, rather they are claiming that these wonders and signs and

114

breakthroughs are a result of the outpouring of a "anointing". And what is the Greek way of saying anointed, or anointing? "Christ" is the Greek way of saying anointing. To receive of Rodney Howard Browne's anointing is another way of saying Rodney Howard Browne's Christ! When they say there is an anointing being poured out in the Toronto Airport Vineyard they are in effect saying, Look there is Christ! The danger is not that of being deceived by false Jesuses; after all most Christians know that the real Jesus has holes in His hands and feet. The warning is "beware of false Christs", false anointings!

John also warned us explicitly when he gave us the test for the Spirit of Truth and the Spirit of error,

Hereby know ye the Spirit of God: Every Spirit that confesseth that Jesus Christ is come in the flesh is of God: and every spirit that denieth that Jesus Christ has come in the flesh is not of God: and this is that Spirit of anti-christ . . ." (I John 4:3-4.)

What are we to be looking for as Christians? Our blessed hope is the appearing of our Lord and Saviour, Jesus Christ! And how is it that he shall return? Bodily, the way he was taken up into heaven, in the flesh, as the angel told the apostles,

Ye men of Galilee, why stand ye gazing up into heaven? This same Jesus, which is taken up from you into heaven, shall so come in like manner as ye have seen him go into heaven. (Acts 1:11.)

John warned us that in some way the Anti-christ will seek to spiritualise Jesus Christ to deceive the world. There is more than one way to do this. To the Jehovah's Witnesses, Christ did not raise bodily from the dead, but in spirit. This is an obviously anti-christ doctrine. To the Mormon's the denial is that Jesus became the Christ, rather than that

Jesus Christ came in the flesh. But to modern Pentecostals and Charismatics the deception is that instead of awaiting the bodily return of Jesus Christ, we are rather to await the outpouring of a new anointing (Christ) which will empower us to become the greatest generation of the church ever!

What we have in this new anointing is a dis-incarnate Christ! It manifests itself in many ways foreign to the Jesus of the Bible. People get drunk in it, soak in it, follow it, tremble in the presence of it, go into trances in the name of it. John Kilpatrick, pastor of the Brownsville Assembly of God, was so drunk in it for several weeks, he had to have help dressing in the morning! He called it "the Glory!" Instead of the patient waiting for the coming of our Lord and Saviour Jesus Christ from heaven, Pentacostals and Charismatics and even many evangelicals have entered into a disincarnate "presence", seeking "it", instead of Him!

Consider the fact that, from the beginning, at both Toronto and Pensacola, "it" was invoked! The true Spirit of Jesus Christ is in the church, praying with and through the church, "Come Lord Jesus!" for the Spirit and the Bride say "Come"! The false spirit, on the contrary is invoked by the command of the newly anointed, "Come! Come Holy Spirit! More! More!" and, as in the testimony of Pastor Benson, the spirit was invoked by simply hitting him in the stomach and shouting in unison, "The Anointing!"

The depersonalised nature of this spirit is further attested to in the testimonies of the many who went to "get it", and perhaps "bring it back to their churches", that others might "soak in it" and perhaps even come under the heavy weight of "it" as Pastor Kilpatrick often has testified.

We need to consider also, how it is that our God changes lives. In the new paradigm, "the River", there seems to be a strong emphasis on change without preaching; instead unbelievers are zapped, as witnessed by the above testimony of Kilpatrick, about the thousands who have been thrown against the wall by the anointing and come up two or three hours later asking what they must do to be saved. In fact there seems almost at times to be an anti-preaching bias. When standing outside, in the depths of the Canadian winter, to interview those waiting for three hours to get into the Toronto Airport Vineyard services in 1995, a good many pastors from around the world were available. Without exception, the constant theme was, "We don't preach anymore, since the Spirit came, we don't need to, the Spirit has taken over."

Ours is the Faith in the *Logos* of God; God has spoken, and by the Word he *"Heals us and delivers us from our destructions". "In the beginning was the Word"* and it is the Truth that shall make men free. The God of the Bible doesn't 'zap' people into conversion, *"The Son of God has come and has given us an understanding . . ." (I John 5:20).*

Whenever God's people are denied a consistent, sound doctrinal diet, they are tempted to resort to symbols: pageants, sensuality and personalities as a golden calf substitute. This explains "Brave Heart" swords, Marches for Jesus, Identificational repentances, symbolic actions such as driving stakes engraved with scriptures at the corners of cities, Spiritual warfare dances with staves and a whole host of other pagan practices currently taking place in Pentecostal and Charismatic churches around the world. When the God of the Bible wants to effect change He presents Truth to the minds and consciences of the people, demanding that they conform to it. It is "Truth that sets free." Paganism and magic are anti-rational and symbolic and are not Christianity.

Perhaps this current explosion of mysticised Christianity represents the failure of Pastors, especially Pentecostals, to feed the church with sound doctrine, after all what are people looking for anyway? I thought we found what we wanted when we came to the Fountain of Living Water, Jesus! Why this restlessness, this openness to anything and everything except sound doctrine? I believe that we are in the time of the famine spoken of by both Amos and Paul,

Behold, the days come saith the Lord God, that I will send a famine in the Land, not a famione of bread, nor a thirst for water, but of hearing the words of the Lord, and they shall wander from sea to sea, and from the North even to the east, they shall run to and fro to seek the Word of the Lord and shall not find it . . . (Amos 8:11-12.)

For the time will come when they shall not endure sound doctrine; but after their own lusts shall they heap to themselves teachers, having itching ears; and they shall turn away their ears from the truth, and shall be turned unto fables. (I Timothy 4:3-4.)

Is there a way back? How do you admit you are wrong after going under the "tunnel of fire"? Worse yet, how can you admit you were decieved when you were the one who formed the tunnel with your "Braveheart" sword? It is because we are often unwilling to be reproached, we want to be great, and regarded as "cutting edge" that we become seduced by all of this. How else could we explain the proud boasting, the swelling prophecies, the desire to have the power to turn stones into bread? *"If we confess our sins, He is faithful and just to forgive us our sins and to cleanse us from all unrighteousness."*

Appendix

The God Chasers Tommy Tenney (Destiny Image)

Tommy Tenney is a third generation United Pentecostal minister who bills himself and his growing following as "God Chasers". He is the author of a best-selling book entitled *The God Chasers*. He has also served as a pastor for ten years and has spent another 17 years as a "revivalist". According to the blurb on the back cover of his recent book, he has been used to both "spark and fuel the fires of revival" . It also states that although "He has experienced the miraculous. . . more importantly he knows the value of intimacy with a humility before God."

The book, *The God Chasers*, is a call to those who consider themselves to be hungry for the manifested presence of God. It begins with a narrative which should strike a chord with those who have been radicalised by experience-based religion à la Toronto and Pensacola. In the chapter entitled "The day I almost caught Him", ("Him" referring to God), Tenney describes a service he held in Houston, Texas, in which upon the reading of II Chronicles 7:14, and an exhortation by the host pastor to "seek God's face rather than just His hand", a loud thunderclap sounded and split the pulpit into two pieces! From there the usual "river" manifestations exploded across the sanctuary, slayings in the spirit, profuse cryings, and even the bodies of businessmen stacked up "like chordwood"!

Businessmen tore their ties off, and they were literally stacked on top of one another, in the most horribly harmonious sound of repentance you ever heard.

By his own confession, Tenney had been up to that point merely a professional revivalist,

We've talked, preached and taught about revival until the church is sick of hearing about it. That's what I did for a living, I preached revivals, or so I thought. Then God broke out of His box and ruined everything when He showed up.

Tenney echoes an earlier prophecy of the late John Wimber, by saying that "God is coming back to repossess His church." But his premise is that the only thing that hinders God from "repossessing His church" is the lack of spiritual hunger, which Tenney and others seem to interpret as a hunger for the "manifested presence" of God. Thus the book, *The God Chasers*, is aimed at those who are,

. . . tired of trying to pass out tracts , knock on doors, and make things happen. . . we've been trying to make things happen for a long time. Now he wants to make it happen! (p.12.)

Part of the problem according to Tenney, comes down to the predictable assertion that too many of us have been "Camped out on some dusty truth known to everyone."

There's the problem: "dusty truth"! But of course Tenney would lead us and guide us into his alternative to "dusty truth", what he calls "Revelation",

The difference between the truth of God and revelation is very simple. Truth is where God has been. Revelation is where God is. Truth is God's tracks. It is His Trail, His path, but it leads to what? It leads to Him. Perhaps the masses of people are happy to know where God's been, but true God Chasers are not content to study God's trail, His truths, they want to know Him. They want to know where He is and what He is doing right now. . . There is a vast difference between present truth and past truth. I am afraid that most of what the church has studied is past truth, and very little of what we know is present truth". (From the introduction.)

Tenney's call for an abandonment of "past truth" in favour of his more relevant "present truth" is far from original. He is only the latest in a long line of teachers who have tapped into the discontentment that many have in this entertainment age, subtly denigrating the sound teaching of the Word of God, in order to promote the latest expression of experienced-based religion. As the children of Israel tired of manna, in their day, the modern children of God "will not endure sound doctrine" either. Tenney, like many others these days, is adept at ridiculing teaching and Bible study, as though they were as irrelevant as a game of "Trivial Pursuit",

It is simply not enough to know about God. We have churches filled with people who can win Bible trivia contests but who don't know Him. (p.3.)

So much for those Christians, off into "dusty truth", enamoured by God's tracks, but what about the New Agers and occultists? Tenney is sure that they have the purest of motives,

You can't tell me they're not hungry for God when they wear crystals around their necks, lay down hundreds of dollars a day to listen to Gurus, and call psychics to the tune of billions of dollars a year. (p.2.)

Of course these pure hearted seekers are only hindered by one obstacle, in their search for God, the church! (I always thought that it was the fact that "there is none that seeks after God", that rather than seeking God, witches and occultists and those who seek fortune tellers were in rebellion to God.)

> They're hungry to hear from something that's beyond themselves, something they are not hearing in the church of today. The bottom line is that people are sick of the church because the church has been somewhat less than the book has advertised." (p.3.)

> Naomi and her family have something in common with the people who leave or totally avoid churches today – they left "that" place and went somewhere else to find bread. I can tell you why people are flocking to the bars, the clubs, and the Psychics by the millions. They are just trying to get by, they are just trying to survive because the church has failed them. They looked, or their parents and friends looked and reported, and the spiritual cupboard was bare" (p.19-20.)

The church is the one forcing people who are earnestly searching for God out into the bars and clubs? What ever happened to *"They knew God but would not glorify Him as God, neither were they thankful . . . therefore they are without excuse"?* Not so according to Tenney, these good-hearted witches and occultists actually came to church but found nothing, therefore they have had no choice but to go into the occult! This kind of accusation will always find a ready audience in our modern "seeker sensitive" world, discontented, and casting about for any scapegoat for their sense of restlessness. The church is at fault!

Between the various personal experiences recounted by Tenney and his attempts at whetting the spiritual appetites which the book calls for, glimpses of the author's theology can be seen. As we have already seen,

122

Tenney holds to a curious view of the Word of God, as being "God's tracks", "where God's been", and "past truth", interesting; but not enough for the "God chasers". Tenney further denigrates the Word of God, and those who would insist on measuring all things by it, in a very unusual and creative way, he calls the Scripture "old love letters", appearing to pay some homage to them, yet at the same time rendering their present application irrelevant.

> I'm afraid we have satiated our hunger for Him by reading old love letters from him to the churches in the epistles of the New Testament. These are good, holy and necessary, but we never have intimacy with Him . . . (p.15.)

Tenney generously concedes that the Scriptures are "good, holy and necessary", but . . . (and there is a world of meaning in that "but") by designating Scripture to the status of "old love letters", he renders them inadequate for present intimacy with God! Picture Paul relegating Scripture to the status of "old love letters"! Jesus never contrasted "intimacy" with God and "power" from God as opposed to Scripture, He equated them! *"Do ye not err? Not knowing the scripture or the power of God?"* Knowing and loving Scripture is the only way to begin to have intimacy with God, not the obstacle to it! Of course there could be a problem of people being "hearers of the Word and not doers of it", but the answer is not to compare Scripture to "old love letters" or worse yet, to relegate scriptural knowledge to "being able to win a Bible Trivia game". What is Tenney promoting? Perhaps the answer to this can be found in the oft-cited nugget of charismatic wisdom,

> . . . A man with experience is never at the mercy of a man with only an argument... If we can lead people into the manifest presence of God, all false theological houses of cards will tumble down. (p.20.)

This saying or some variation of it is basically the underlying assumption of the entire "River" revival, that experience supercedes "doctrine", and that the Word alone is insufficient for relationship with God.

Did the apostles believe this way? Did they ever "split pulpits"? Did they constantly contrast Truth and intimacy? Peter had the ultimate sensual religious encounter, He saw the transfigured Jesus, but rather than contrast his experience on the loly mountain with those who are still "stuck in some dusty truth", Peter commended us to the *"more sure Word of Prophecy, which you would do well to take heed unto"*. Peter never held a laughing revival, nor did Paul ever refer to Himself as God's bartender. James never saw the need to put loaves of bread on the altar so that it could soak up the anointing.

Nor did the apostles ever conduct the kind of spiritual warfare Tenney and others proclaim in the name of "Taking their cities for God".

> I am after cities . . . Once while preaching at a conference . . . in Portland, Oregan, I heard him [Frank Dimazio] mention something that caught my attention. He said that a number of pastors in the Portland area had united together to drive some stakes in the ground at strategic places around the perimeter of their region and the city and at every major intersection. The process took them hours because they also prayed over those stakes, as they were physical symbols marking a spiritual declaration and demarcation line. I felt the stirring of the Holy Spirit so I said, "Frank, if you'll provide the stakes, then I'll go to the cities I feel called to and help the pastors stake out that territory for God." (p.102-103.)

Is this another Toronto or Pensacola? I think Tenney and I would probably disagree. I would say that this "intimacy" that is being sought is of the same nature as that "presence" that pilgrims to Toronto and

124

Pensacola have sought encounters with. Tenney seems to allude to these earlier revivals, on p.21, as being somewhat less than what he is promoting,

> People don't sense God's presence at our gatherings because it is just not there sufficiently to register on our gauges . . . when people get just a little touch of God mixed with a lot of something that is not God, it inoculates them against the real thing. Once they've been inoculated by a crumb of God's presence, then when they say "God is really here", they say, "No, I've been there, done that. I bought the T-shirt, and I didn't find Him, it really didn't work for me." The problem was that God was there alright, but not enough of Him. There was no experience of meeting Him at the Damascus road. There was no undeniable, overwhelming sense of His manifested presence.

Tenney may well have made a point without realising it. He acknowledges that the experienced-based revivals of our day (with their sensual encounters with "the presence") tend eventually towards a "been there done that" attitude, as repeated mystical experiences lead into a kind of spiritual "Law of diminishing returns", but the answer, according to Tenney, is more of "it". Toronto and Pensacola were only crumbs, there's more of it in a purer form. Rodney Howard Browne held forth to those who were weary of "dead religion" a fresh touch of God, a drink on the "new wine". Toronto came along and offered those same people an opportunity to "soak in" the manifested anointing of God. Pensacola, which in spite of denials to the contrary, is directly descended from the Toronto Blessing (Steve Hill, bringing "it" back with him from Holy Trinity church, Brompton, the Toronto Church of England) offered a purer touch revival than Toronto, putting more emphasis on repentance. But to Tenney, these were just crumbs. What does he offer? More of God? These are all the same claims, the same cliches, the same criticisms of doctrine, and even in many cases the same denigrations of the Word. I predict that, as in the other "waves", this also will leave many emptier even than they were before. Unfortunately this will only open them up to the next excursion into mystical, experienced-based religion.

Orthodox Christianity has held that true Hunger for God is valid and can be validly met through seeking Him, fasting, prayer, a renewal of obedience to Him, a going back to wherever it was that we left Him. "Signs and wonders" are not God nor do they satisfy. Even fantastic signs such as splitting pulpits, slaying whole crowds in the spirit, businessmen laying around like 'chordwood', none of this necessarily has anything to do with truly hungering for God.

Finally, is *The God Chasers* really about the kind of hunger for God that perhaps Tozer wrote of, or Spurgeon, Wesley, Nee and the other giants of the Faith of days gone by? You be the judge. But lest there be any doubt that some other kind of hunger is at work here, consider that the last page of this Destiny Image book is an advertising page featuring the full line of *God Chasers* products. The *God Chasers hat* is available for a mere $17.99, the *God Chaser shirt* is available in four sizes for a mere $16.99, and for those who truly want to attest to this new hunger, the *God Chasers licence plate* is available for a mere $6.99!

Pastor Bill Randles, Cedar Rapids, Iowa